Genuine Risk

Genuine Risk

by HALLIE McEVOY

THOROUGHBRED
Legends®
No. 20

ECLIPSE
PRESS

Lexington, Kentucky

Library of Congress Control Number: 2002114038

ISBN 1-58150-092-0

Printed in The United States
First Edition: June 2003

Distributed to the trade by
National Book Network
4720-A Boston Way
Lanham, MD 20706
1.800.462.6420

a division of
Blood-Horse Publications
PUBLISHERS SINCE 1916

GENUINE RISK

CONTENTS

INTRODUCTION

$20 To Win

I have always liked fillies, and that devotion deepened thanks to a special autumn afternoon at Belmont Park in 1973. For my thirteenth birthday my parents took me to the Beldame Stakes. It was the first race I ever attended even though we lived a scant thirty minutes from Belmont. To this day I am still lured by that fabled track, and any time I am near New York, I can almost hear the hoof beats from the backstretch.

That day Desert Vixen defeated my idol, Susan's Girl, who finished third while trying to win her second Beldame in a row. As those two came mincing back to the grandstand covered in dirt, I felt nothing could be finer than the look of a Thoroughbred after a job well done. Although I did not know it at the time, that race would become known as one of the greatest meetings of fillies and mares ever.

But that race affected me on a deeper level. I was now totally and hopelessly in love with the fairer sex on the racetrack. Fillies and mares became my obsession, and to this day I'd rather watch a maiden special weight for fillies than a stakes race full of good colts.

Two years later in 1975, I sat in the stands at Belmont for the ill-fated match race between the filly Ruffian and the colt Foolish Pleasure. I watched in disbelief as the valiant Ruffian pulled into the lead, took a bad step, and broke down, while Foolish Pleasure raced on alone. It seemed so unfair to see trainer LeRoy Jolley in the winner's circle with the colt, as the suffering Ruffian was loaded into a horse ambulance and taken off the track. For reasons unclear to me now as then, I held it against Jolley, though the tragedy had nothing to do with him.

In 1979 I was old enough to drive myself to the track. Friends I'd made at Belmont spoke of a talented two-year-old chestnut filly, whose blazed face was in front in each of her four starts that year. By the spring of 1980, that filly, Genuine Risk, found an opening on the outside and darted her way into my heart.

It was during that spring I changed my tune about Jolley. Following Genuine Risk's career through the *Daily*

Racing Form and whispered words from the backstretch, I watched as Jolley carefully brought along the speedy Genuine Risk. Despite some misgivings and miscommunications with the owners, Bert and Diana Firestone, about the correct path to take for the filly, Jolley had Genuine Risk tuned to perfection for the first Saturday in May.

On Friday, May 2, 1980, I made my way into an off-track betting parlor in Huntington, New York, to put twenty dollars on Genuine Risk for the Kentucky Derby. To call this particular betting parlor a dive would have been charitable. Walking briskly past the paid companions loitering at the door, I clutched my money. I quickly realized not many college girls frequented the parlor, and even fewer made the mistake of waltzing in wearing half-chaps and paddock boots (I had just come from exercising Thoroughbreds at a local farm). Having never been inside a betting parlor, I had no idea what to expect.

Soon, I had unwittingly become the center of unwanted attention. "Hey, girlie, who you putting your money on for the Derby?" asked a timeworn man in a porkpie hat. Scattered about him were *Daily Racing Forms* and a few *Blood-Horse* magazines. His cigar burned

lazily toward the inoperative ceiling fan, and it was clear that he spent every day in the same spot. "You gallop ponies? Call me Big Bob. Sit down and talk to me," he commanded in a gruff way.

Soon I found out Bob only smoked Cuban cigars: "Don't ask how I get them, girlie, but they're worth it." He also had seen every big horse of the twentieth century run, including Man o' War, Count Fleet, Citation, Nashua, Dr. Fager, Kelso, and all the greats of the 1970s — Riva Ridge, Secretariat, Affirmed, Seattle Slew, and Spectacular Bid. Not once did he mention a filly's name or mare's name in the bunch.

He was studying the charts for the next day's main event, and nothing was making sense to him. "The charts usually speak to me, but I can't figure this one out. How much you betting and on who?" he asked in a bemused way.

Feeling put on the spot, I stammered, "Twenty dollars on Genuine Risk."

Bob's eyebrows shot up under his hat. "You're going with the filly, huh? You really think she can do it?" I nodded, afraid to open my mouth. "Well, girlie, then I'll bet on the filly, too."

At that point I realized Big Bob had dismissed me. The other parlor denizens seemed to favor Jaklin Klugman and Rockhill Native and didn't give the filly much chance. I wondered if I should have kept my opinion to myself. I walked to the counter and put down my hard-earned money with a sense of guilt, knowing that I should probably be saving it for books for the fall semester. But I had a gut feeling about Genuine Risk.

On Monday, May 5, I went back to collect my winnings. My twenty dollars had yielded close to $150 — way less than the $286 I would have won on track (there was a cap on OTB payouts at the time) but a small fortune for a college girl in 1980.

Big Bob was sitting in his usual spot. He waved me over and cleared a place for me. "You made me a lot of money, girlie," he said and punctuated each word with the tip of his cigar. "A lot of money." He pressed an envelope into my hand and waved me away. Outside, I discovered the envelope contained a five hundred dollar bill.

I found out later that between the betting parlor and a few bookies Bob had laid down two thousand dollars on Genuine Risk. It was rumored that he had pulled in close to $200,000. I went back the next day to thank

him for the cash. He barely looked up. "What gift?" he said as he studied that day's *Form*. "Let's not be talking about it." I smiled and left, never to return.

But a part of my heart would forever stay with Genuine Risk, and I fretted over each of her subsequent starts like a mother hen. The Preakness debacle, where she was mugged, continues to haunt me and is still argued about in both boardrooms and tack rooms. Her gutsy performance in the Belmont, never giving up, showed what true grit she possessed. Through her career, and despite the fact that many horsemen discount fillies and mares, my dedication never wavered.

It appears that fillies and mares are held to a different standard; Genuine Risk only ranks ninety-first on the list in *Thoroughbred Champions: Top 100 Racehorses of the 20th Century* (The Blood-Horse Inc., 1999). To accomplish what she did, finishing first in the Derby and second in the Preakness and Belmont, it would seem she should be a bit higher on the list.

Other people agree. In researching this book, I found that dozens of horsemen and journalists shared Genuine Risk memories and press clippings. What would have compelled so many diverse individuals to squirrel away faded newspaper accounts? It could only be the love of a fine athlete and the confidence that their adoration was not misplaced.

Part of the drama of the Genuine Risk story is the champion's difficulty in producing offspring. It took eleven years and countless heartaches before she had a live foal.

When Genuine Risk finally delivered the aptly named Genuine Reward in 1993, Three Chimneys Farm in Kentucky received hundreds of cards and letters for the new mother and her colt.

It is, however, as a racehorse and symbol of women's liberation, that Genuine Risk will best be remembered. The 1970s saw the rise of women in the workforce and in politics. Genuine Risk embodied the hopes and dreams of so many of these women who wanted it all, a successful career and equality in a man's world. For a lot of these women, motherhood came much later as it did for Genuine Risk.

In 1980 the editors of *Harper's Bazaar* named the top-seven female achievers of the year: dancer Twyla Tharp, U.S. Department of Education Secretary Shirley Hufstedler, conductor Sarah Caldwell, columnist Jane

Bryant Quinn, television personality Sue Simmons, New York City Council President Carol Bellamy, and Genuine Risk. It made perfect sense that Genuine Risk was included on the list as she was a female role model and leader.

Genuine Risk became only the second filly to win the Kentucky Derby — Regret had accomplished the task sixty-five years earlier. Winning the Run for the Roses just a few years after the celebrated Billie Jean King and Bobby Riggs tennis match, Genuine Risk made a strong statement as to the equality of females in sports — whether wearing tennis shoes or horseshoes.

Hallie McEvoy
Bolton Valley, Vermont, 2003

GENUINE RISK

CHAPTER 1

Beginner's Luck

The chances of the average Thoroughbred owner breeding a Kentucky Derby winner are very slim. Horsemen spend years breeding the best to the best and never come close to success in the classic races. For Mrs. G. Watts Humphrey Jr. to breed Genuine Risk in her first independent foray into breeding, the odds must have been infinitesimal.

Born Sally Schriber, the future Mrs. Humphrey grew up in Southern California. Her father being in the steel business, Sally wasn't raised around horses, though she later owned a Quarter Horse while at school in Arizona and hoped to marry someone who loved horses as much as she did. When she met Yale student G. Watts Humphrey while attending college at Briarcliff College in Briarcliff Manor, New York, she found the perfect match. He was a product of a horse racing family. And

Sally, who had never been to a horse race, was quickly introduced to that world when they honeymooned in Saratoga Springs, New York.

Watts showed horses in his youth and was connected to Thoroughbred racing and breeding through his grandfather, George M. Humphrey, and his great aunt, Mrs. Parker Poe. George Humphrey, who founded the National Steel Corporation, bought Kentucky's Whileaway Farm in 1957. An apt student of bloodlines, he started his operation with quality broodmares, including Nalee and Searching. George eventually bred such stakes winners as Nalees Man, Dinner Partner, and Zabriskie Point. Life at Whileaway Farm was far removed from the stress of his positions as secretary of the U.S. Department of the Treasury under Dwight D. Eisenhower and head of the family steel business.

On his mother's side of the family, Watts' great aunt, Elizabeth Poe (then Miss Elizabeth Ireland), bought Shawnee Farm near Harrodsburg, Kentucky, in 1939. The farm already had a storied history, having belonged to Colonel Jack Chinn, father of renowned racing figure Colonel Phil T. Chinn (who was born on the farm). Jack Chinn later christened the property Leonatus Farm after

the 1883 Kentucky Derby winner whom he raced.
Starting in the 1940s, Mrs. Poe sold yearlings at auction,
beginning a family trend of breeding to sell. Among the
best horses Mrs. Poe bred were Prince Tenderfoot,
Young Emperor, Bornastar, and Globemaster.

As a young man, Watts became involved with the
family's Thoroughbred business and inherited
Shawnee Farm from Mrs. Poe upon her death in 1978.

After the Humphreys' marriage and the birth of their
two daughters and son, Sally asked for a special thirti-
eth birthday present, her own broodmare. Watts happi-
ly complied, giving her thirty thousand dollars to spend
at the 1975 Keeneland November breeding stock sale,
but on the condition that Sally go through the catalog,
pick out mares based on pedigree, and then go look at
their conformation. The decision was all hers. For Sally,
the opportunity was both exciting and daunting.

After looking at the catalog, Sally examined the
mares. She found only one she liked on pedigree and
conformation: Virtuous, Hip #147. Sally knew this
Gallant Man mare was the one she was after.

"Virtuous was a very correct, solid, and nice mare.
She was also very sweet. I wouldn't call her fancy, but

she was very correct," she recalled. "From what I was told, she looked a lot like Gallant Man."

Gallant Man was part of the outstanding crop of 1954 that included Bold Ruler, Round Table, and Iron Liege. An imported son of Migoli, Gallant Man was a top-notch handicapper, finishing second by a nose in the 1957 Kentucky Derby (some believe because of a riding error on the part of jockey Bill Shoemaker) and later winning the Belmont Stakes, Travers, and Jockey Club Gold Cup. His dam, Majideh, was by the legendary Mahmoud, winner of the 1936 Epsom Derby.

Virtuous' female line was equally regal. Her grand-dam, Auld Alliance (by Brantome, the 1934 Prix de l'Arc de Triomphe winner, out of Iona, by Hyperion) was the dam of 1959 Kentucky Derby winner Tomy Lee. The female line traces further back to the taproot mare Paraffin, whose daughter Illuminata produced 1894 Epsom Derby winner Ladas and 1897 One Thousand Guineas winner Chelandry (seventh dam of Virtuous).

Sally also liked the racing form Virtuous had shown in France. Virtuous, bred by Mereworth Farm in Kentucky, had been consigned by her breeder to the 1972 Saratoga yearling sale and bought by John A. Bell

III of the Cromwell Bloodstock Agency for $22,000. As a two-year-old in 1973, the Gallant Man filly won one race in four starts and finished second in the Prix de la Vallee d'Auge at Deauville for owner Frederic Papert. At three she ran five times, winning once.

In 1975 Virtuous returned to America and raced a single time as a four-year-old, finishing off the board. After her racing career ended, she was bred to Stage Door Johnny and consigned to the 1975 November Keeneland sale by Jonabell Farm for Papert.

Sally was supposed to do her own bidding at the auction, but she shook so much that Watts took over. He purchased Virtuous for his wife for $31,500. Even with the excitement over and the mare hers, Sally was still so shaken she couldn't sign the ticket. Her dutiful husband took care of that important detail.

Sally's game plan was to sell the Stage Door Johnny foal and all subsequent babies. In the spring of 1976, Virtuous foaled a healthy colt. At the Keeneland September yearling sale the following year, Sally sold the colt through the Shawnee Farm consignment to Dogwood Farm, agent. The $24,500 fetching price for a first foal showed Sally had a good eye for broodmares

and pedigrees. Shin splints prevented the colt, later named Masher, from ever racing.

For the next mating Sally chose Exclusive Native. "Watts advised me and really picked out this nick," she said. "Exclusive Native was a strong and upcoming stallion with a good classic pedigree going for him."

Louis Wolfson, the owner of Harbor View Farm, bred and raced Exclusive Native, who was sired by the speed influence Raise a Native. A son of Native Dancer and the Case Ace mare Raise You, Raise a Native was a brilliant juvenile, winning all four starts before injury forced him into early retirement. Even so, he still earned champion two-year-old colt honors for 1963. As a sire he was even more brilliant, siring seventy-eight stakes winners, including Mr. Prospector, who became a great sire in his own right; dual classic winner Majestic Prince; English champion juvenile Crowned Prince; and Alydar, an outstanding racehorse and sire.

Exclusive Native's dam, Exclusive, was by the 1942 Kentucky Derby and Belmont winner Shut Out and out of the Pilate mare Good Example. Exclusive won four of ten races and produced four other stakes winners, including 1970 Prioress Stakes winner Exclusive

Dancer (by Native Dancer). Exclusive Dancer became the dam of Travers winner General Assembly and multiple grade III winner Expressive Dance, both of whom raced for the Firestone family. Expressive Dance produced grade I winner Chief Honcho, who later was to share another familial connection to Genuine Risk.

Exclusive Native raced for two seasons, winning four of thirteen starts, including the Sanford Stakes at two and the Arlington Classic Stakes at three. He entered stud in 1969 and his first runners hit the track in 1972, including Our Native who went on to win the 1973 Flamingo Stakes and Monmouth Invitational Handicap, both grade Is, and run third to Secretariat in the Kentucky Derby and Preakness.

At the time Watts and Sally decided on the mating to Exclusive Native, another of the stallion's offspring was waiting in the wings for his debut. Affirmed, then a yearling, would take center stage of the racing world for the next two years, besting rival Alydar for juvenile champion honors in 1977, then gritting out the Triple Crown victory in 1978, again over Alydar.

But with Exclusive Native still trying to make his way to the top of the sire ranks, the Humphreys could

only hope the mating with Virtuous would pan out.

"I'd like to say I knew exactly what we were getting, but that's not true," Sally reminisced. "I wish I could say I knew we were breeding a Kentucky Derby winner. Honestly, it was beginner's luck! She (Genuine Risk) was the first horse I ever bred myself; it's been all downhill or uphill from there, depending on how you look at it."

On February 15, 1977, Virtuous foaled a large chestnut filly with a broad blaze on her face. Despite the foal's size, it was an easy foaling for farm manager Al Cofield (who began at Shawnee in 1955) and his assistant R.T. Blackburn.

During the summer the Exclusive Native filly was weaned from her mother, who was now in foal to Silent Screen. The chestnut filly ran with the other weanlings at Shawnee Farm and acquired no nicknames. She was just known as the "Virtuous filly."

By the spring of 1978, the Shawnee Farm crew was preparing the yearling filly for the Fasig-Tipton summer sale in Kentucky. No one could have known then what a bright future was in store for the Virtuous filly, nor that at the auction, a fourteen-year-old boy would pick her out and urge his father to buy her.

CHAPTER 2

A Youthful Veteran Of The Sales

By the time he was fourteen, Matthew "Matt" Firestone was a veteran of Thoroughbred auctions. His interest in horses came as little surprise to his father Bertram "Bert" Firestone and stepmother, Diana, who had met at a horse show and who owned Catoctin Stud near Waterford, Virginia. Diana was the daughter and heiress of John Seward Johnson of Johnson & Johnson, the giant health care products manufacturer and pharmaceuticals company. Bert had made his money in both real estate and horse racing.

Matt was one of three sons Bert brought from his previous marriage to his new one with Diana, who had one son and two daughters from her own previous marriage. The couple also had a child together, Alison, in 1976 when Matt was twelve.

Of all the children, Matt inherited the racing gene.

He read and understood race charts and the *Daily Racing Form* by the time he was seven, an age when he began accompanying his father to auctions. Matt would often assist his father by asking for horses to be taken out of their stalls to be inspected. By the time Matt was ten, he was avidly foxhunting. Most of young Matt's friends either rode or were involved in racing.

At age fifteen, Matt began eventing, a highly challenging horse sport that involves dressage, riding cross-country, and show jumping. In 1986 Matt was picked by the U.S. Equestrian Team to represent America at the World Championships in Poland. He and his teammates brought home silver medals. A broken arm in 1988 derailed his plans to ride in the Olympics.

Although Bert and Diana enjoyed the thrill of showing hunters and jumpers, their partnership truly shined in the world of Thoroughbred racing. The couple campaigned such superb horses as General Assembly, Honest Pleasure, Optimistic Gal, What a Summer, King's Company, Exclusive Dancer, and Red Alert.

Despite their prominence in the Thoroughbred world, the Firestones shunned the limelight and any display of ostentation. Intensely private, Bert and Diana centered their life around family and horses.

The Firestone family had a good record in picking out horses at auction that would pay them back in the winner's circle. Optimistic Gal was bought for $55,000 and went on to earn $686,861. It took just $45,000 to acquire Honest Pleasure who brought home $839,997, almost won the Kentucky Derby, and was syndicated for more than five million dollars.

Diana paid a bit more for the brilliant filly What a Summer. Purchased as a four-year-old at the 1977 Hialeah winter mixed sale for the top price of $275,000, the Maryland-bred filly went on to win an Eclipse Award, the Oscar of horse racing, as the nation's leading sprinter that year. Eclipse voters may have favored What a Summer for the commanding way she galloped to victory in the Fall Highweight Handicap at Belmont Park carrying 134 pounds.

But Matt actually picked out Genuine Risk, the horse that would bring the Firestone family its greatest fame. The young teenager accompanied the Catoctin Stud manager, Marvin Greene, to the 1978 Fasig-Tipton Kentucky July yearling sale.

Matt remembers the sale well. "My father would go

through the catalog prior to each auction and pick out horses we would look at. For some reason the Exclusive Native—Virtuous filly was not on our original list to inspect at the Fasig-Tipton sale."

Matt knew the types of pedigrees they were looking for and had noticed her pedigree at dinner the night before the sale. He thought she'd fit in with their program. "Dad, I think we missed one; you should look at her," the young horseman said. The filly's sire had no doubt caught his eye.

Just months before, Affirmed, a son of Exclusive Native, had gutted out a tough victory in the Triple Crown races.

Genuine Risk came very close to being passed over by the Firestones. If Matt had not been looking beyond the Firestones' original list, Genuine Risk might have gone to other owners. Fortunately, he convinced his father to look at the filly before the sale commenced.

"Matt came to me before the start of the sale and said he had a horse he wanted me to see," Bert remembered. "The sale was getting ready to start, and I did not think we would be able to see her as they (the consignors) had stopped showing horses."

But the Firestones did get to see the chestnut filly, and they agreed to bid to about $40,000. Matt sat next to his parents and did the bidding. Bert had no qualms letting his son handle the purchase.

"Matt had been going to the sales since he was young. He knew the nice horses from the bad horses," said Bert. When the gavel fell, the Virtuous filly belonged to the Firestones for $32,000.

"No one looks at a yearling and says 'this one will win the Derby,' " reflected Matt twenty-five years later. "Everyone still makes a big deal about me picking her out when I was so young. I was always a part of the operation, and Genuine Risk just happened to be one of the few at that time that I looked at independently. I was always involved in the team effort at the sales."

Bert remembers it a little bit differently. "When we bought her, Matt asked me if I thought she would win a stakes, and I said we needed to worry about winning a maiden race first. I had a fleeting thought, 'suppose she wins the Derby,' during that conversation. I have always remembered that."

The chestnut filly would soon need a name. Nothing catchy immediately jumped out at the family, which

liked to use names derived from bloodlines.

The family was vacationing in Sun Valley, Idaho, and the issue of names came up for the young horses in the stable. "We decided that racing was a 'genuine risk' and that is how we came up with her name," Bert stated. "We never really called her by a nickname. 'Genny' was often used by the public and the media." Even though it had nothing to do with her bloodlines, the name Genuine Risk just felt right to the Firestones.

One thing was certain: Genuine Risk would race listed as owned by Diana. At the time, all the fillies in the stable raced under Diana's name while the colts raced under Bert's. All raced in the green-and-white Firestone silks although the jockey's caps had slight differences: Bert had a green and white quartered cap, while Diana's was solid green.

In the fall of her yearling year, Genuine Risk was broken to saddle and bridle by Catoctin Stud employees John "Buck" Moore, Randolph Blunt, and Harris Tracy. She was not an easy pupil. "Genuine Risk was a bit on the tough side to break," remembered Buck, who first started working for Diana in 1962.

"But that's the same toughness that makes a good

racehorse. Although she was tough, she never tried to hurt you. She just made it clear that you couldn't push her around. You'd be going along pretty well and then she'd throw in a buck. She was fun to break and really acted more like an average colt than a filly."

During her early training, the filly was especially hard to long-line a training method used for young horses. Long canvas lines are attached to the bit and the horse is driven from behind by the trainer, much as if a carriage were behind the horse. Two shorter side reins are attached from the bit to a strap around the horse's back and belly. These side reins help teach the horse how to carry his head and neck. The trainer gives voice cues to tell the horse what is expected of him.

Horses that are trained in this manner prior to having a rider on their back are generally more tractable and easy to break to saddle.

"The first time we long-lined her, it took two hours. The next time we got it down to an hour."

At the time he broke her, Buck didn't have an inkling of what a great racehorse Genuine Risk would become. "I wish I could say I knew that she was going to be special, but I really had no clue. I just knew she was a filly who was aggressive, could fight back, and was tough."

As the filly continued to grow and mature, so too did the relationship between her future trainer and jockey, LeRoy Jolley and Jacinto Vasquez. Although their names will be forever linked in racing history through Foolish Pleasure and Genuine Risk, the two could not have had more dissimilar beginnings.

LeRoy's parents were instrumental in his training career. His father, Moody Jolley, had been a jockey, exercise rider, valet, agent, breeder, owner, and trainer over his long career. In the 1950s Moody trained such famous horses as Round Table, Doubledogdare, Delta, Monarchy, Bayou, and Nadir, and his owners included Claiborne Farm and Harry Guggenheim. Moody could be difficult and curt, but there was not much he hadn't done on the track.

Born in Hot Springs, Arkansas, in 1938, LeRoy began walking hots for his father at the tender age of seven on the New York and Florida circuits. During his late teen years LeRoy apprenticed with Moody for two years, and although the young man detoured to the University of Miami for a year, there was never any doubt in LeRoy's mind that he would follow in his father's footsteps.

LeRoy received his trainer's license in 1958 at the age of nineteen. But just because he was starting out on his own didn't mean the family support ended. Somnus, LeRoy's first horse in the winner's circle, was bred by Moody and owned by his mother. Within five years LeRoy had saddled his first horse for the Kentucky Derby, the Claiborne Farm-bred Ridan, owned by his mother, John Greer, and Ernest Woods. Ridan had been picked out by Moody, who named the colt after Claiborne's homebred Nadir. Because Ridan resembled the older horse whom Moody had trained to champion two-year-old colt honors in 1957, Moody reversed the spelling of Nadir's name.

Ridan became the younger Jolley's first stakes winner, going undefeated in seven starts at two and being named co-champion two-year-old colt for 1961. Jolley was a youthful twenty-three at the time. In 1962 Ridan captured the Hibiscus Stakes before galloping to victory in the Florida Derby and then the Blue Grass Stakes. Ridan finished third in the 1962 Kentucky Derby and second in the Preakness Stakes and went on to earn

$635,074 over his career, a huge sum in the early 1960s.

By the 1970s LeRoy had hit his stride as a trainer, and in 1972 he added the Firestones to his list of owners. Just three years after that, LeRoy joined the select list of Kentucky Derby-winning trainers with John L. Greer's Foolish Pleasure, another horse his father had assisted in choosing. That same year Honest Pleasure was named champion two-year-old colt for the Firestones, and the following year Honest Pleasure finished a game second in the Derby.

To the press, LeRoy, like his father, could be at turns charming or difficult and was called "irascible" by most who knew the lean and handsome young man. As a trainer he was so consumed with his horses and their health and well being, he could forget niceties.

Up to Moody's death in 1976, father and son remained close. They conferred on every detail, large and small, of their horses together. According to Billy Reed in a 1980 article in the Louisville *Courier-Journal*, LeRoy keenly felt his father's death, missing their conversations and his words of wisdom. "If you know that area code, I sure wish you'd give it to me," he said. "I miss him very, very much."

While a horse trainer's life is never what the outside world would consider secure, LeRoy's entry into racing was backed by his parents. Jacinto Vasquez's life, however, couldn't have been more different.

At age twelve Jacinto decided to run away from rural Las Tablas, Panama. According to an account in Jane Schwartz' *Ruffian: Burning from the Start*, Jacinto's mother had died when he was a small child, leaving behind ten children and her husband, a farmer. There was not much left in Las Tablas for Jacinto, as he didn't want to farm, so he made his way to Remon Racetrack in Panama City and found a job grooming horses despite his small stature and young age. To get into the track, he had climbed a fence and snuck in.

Braulio Baeza was just four years older than Jacinto and already making a name for himself as a jockey on the Panama racing circuit. Jacinto watched admiringly as Baeza left the competition in his wake and boldly forged ahead to America, where he would change the face of racing by becoming one of the first South American riders to make it big in the States. Jacinto dreamed of being a jockey like Baeza and worked hard to improve his riding.

In 1960, at the age of sixteen, Jacinto landed in the United States and tried to make a go of the jockey's life. Due to his immaturity, wild nature, and tendency toward rough riding, he bounced from track to track. From Ak-Sar-Ben in Nebraska to Fair Grounds in Louisiana, he tried to find his niche. Eventually, he broke into the tough Kentucky circuit and also rode in New York, Illinois, New Jersey, and Delaware. By the early 1970s he had settled in New York and made his way to the top jockey ranks.

Part of the positive change for Jacinto came from the stabilizing force of his agent, Harold "Fats" Wiscman. A rarity of body size at the racetrack, Fats stood more than six feet tall and easily weighed more than three hundred pounds. Under Fats' sizeable wing, Jacinto gradually became a dedicated jockey. Over the years Fats had represented such riders as Hall of Famer Walter Blum, whose top mounts included Gun Bow, Pass Catcher, Straight Deal, and Affectionately, but his successful partnership with Jacinto was perhaps Fats' greatest accomplishment as an agent.

LeRoy first used Jacinto as a jockey in New Jersey and Chicago, Illinois, right after Jacinto had arrived in the States. Early on, LeRoy spotted Jacinto's potential and stuck with him through the years. By the time Jacinto rode Foolish Pleasure to victory in the 1975 Derby for LeRoy, the Panamanian was considered one of the greats of the sport. In less than twenty years Jacinto had worked his way up from poverty to a very comfortable life. He was living the American dream. And, through a strange twist of fate, he and his wife, Patricia, bought a house in Garden City, Long Island, right across the street from his childhood idol, Braulio Baeza.

Jacinto was also the main jockey for the great filly Ruffian. It was Fats who persuaded trainer Frank Whiteley to put Jacinto on Ruffian. The unbeaten filly had made short work of her rivals through the Filly Triple Crown (now called the Triple Tiara) races of the Acorn, Mother Goose, and Coaching Club American Oaks in New York.

When a match race was proposed between Foolish Pleasure and Ruffian, Jacinto was in the unenviable position of having to choose between them. Despite the hard feelings he knew it might cause him with LeRoy, he picked Ruffian. All along, LeRoy insisted to the media that he would continue to use Jacinto as a jockey after the match was run.

LeRoy decided on Braulio as the rider for Foolish Pleasure. So the two men, who came from humble beginnings in Panama, would be aboard the two speed-iest horses in America for the match race. What promised to be one of racing's most exciting events turned to disaster when Ruffian shattered a leg and blindly continued to run. Jacinto managed to pull her up before she fell, but she ultimately could not be saved.

After the tragedy of that race, Jacinto went back to riding for LeRoy. He thought of Ruffian often but looked to the future. Soon there would be another filly that would steal the hearts of a nation, and Jacinto would be in the irons for the ride.

CHAPTER 3

A Perfect Season

I n late 1978 Genuine Risk was shipped to Hialeah
with her other young stablemates to begin more
serious work at the track. Although she trained well,
she did not stand out in a crowd. "She was always a
nice filly, one of several very nice fillies I was lucky to
have that year," LeRoy recalled.

The trainer had planned to start the two-year-old in
her first race that summer, but bucked shins, a common
ailment in young racehorses, forced him to postpone
her debut until the fall.

As her first start neared, Genuine Risk was assigned
to the capable hands of Jack Jackson, known to all as
Jackson, a groom who had worked for the Jolley family
for many years. Jackson had groomed for LeRoy's uncle
Tom and his father Moody before joining LeRoy's staff.

Jackson was known for his easy manner with horses and the steady speed at which he worked. Though Genuine Risk was not high strung, Jolley had given Jackson many horses that were.

"I've had horses come in who were upset or nervous, and I'd assign Jackson to them," LeRoy said. "Within a week or ten days, the horses would calm down and become better horses. That's a gift."

John Nazareth, a former jockey with a great sense of pace, became the filly's steady exercise rider. Both Jackson and John were assisted by groom and exercise rider Luis Ortiz.

John accompanied Genuine Risk to New York when LeRoy shipped her there for the fall racing season. Shortly before her first start, she proved herself as more than just a nice filly. With John in the irons, and her stablemate Cybele (also owned by Diana) running alongside her, Genuine Risk put in an impressive work right before her first start.

"She went five-eighths of a mile in :59 or :58 4/5," said LeRoy. "I knew then that she was going to be a good one."

He entered Genuine Risk in a six and a half-furlong, $15,000 maiden special weight for fillies at Belmont

Park on September 30, 1979. Jacinto Vasquez was aboard the chestnut filly for her debut. Rain that day had made the track sloppy, but it didn't seem to matter to Genuine Risk. Carrying 118 pounds, she broke toward the back of the pack but steadily moved up over the sloppy surface. She gradually overtook the leaders and won going away by one and three-quarters lengths. The mud-covered winner completed the race in a respectable 1:18 and was met in the winner's circle by a beaming Diana and Bert.

Just two races later, Cybele, a two-year-old daughter of Cyane, went to the post in another $15,000 maiden special weight for fillies. Like Genuine Risk, Cybele came home in front, and once again, Diana and Bert made the happy trek to the winner's circle.

In an odd quirk of fate, one of Genuine Risk's future Kentucky Derby competitors was also running that day. The little gelding Rockhill Native ran in the eighth race, the $50,000, grade II Cowdin Stakes. Carrying the high weight of 122 pounds, Rockhill Native went off at odds of 3-10 and didn't disappoint his backers. He galloped home on top, with another Derby hopeful Koluctoo Bay just behind him.

LeRoy liked Genuine Risk's performance and the way she was handled by Vasquez, who would ride her in two more starts that year. A little more than two weeks later, on October 18 at Aqueduct, Genuine Risk ran in an allowance race on a fast track that she obviously relished. This time she broke better and pushed the pace over the mile distance, finishing on top by seven and a quarter lengths in 1:36 2/5.

Clearly it was time to move the filly up in class. Aqueduct's $50,000-added Tempted Stakes at a mile on November 5 seemed the perfect opportunity to confirm whether she was stakes material. Carrying 114 pounds over a fast track, Genuine Risk blew by the competition and finished in front of Street Ballet by three lengths.

Genuine Risk's performance impressed her jockey enough that he told Diana that the filly could "beat the colts," as Diana later related to *The Blood-Horse*.

With a three-for-three season going for her, Genuine Risk now had the media's attention. Some writers wondered whether this filly could take the New York Filly Triple Crown and if she were in the same league as Ruffian. LeRoy realized the filly still had a lot to prove before comparisons like that could be made.

Just twelve days after the Tempted, LeRoy entered her in the $75,000-added, grade II Demoiselle Stakes at Aqueduct. The race would test Genuine Risk at a longer distance, a mile and one-eighth, and with a new jockey, Laffit Pincay Jr. Jacinto was not on board due to an alleged disagreement with LeRoy.

Genuine Risk carried 116 pounds, five pounds less than the talented Quadrangle filly, Smart Angle. At the break Tash and Spruce Pine went to the lead. Genuine Risk and Smart Angle stayed just behind the leaders until late in the backstretch when Smart Angle dropped back to sixth as the field bunched. With a brilliant three-wide move in the turn, Genuine Risk took the lead at the head of the stretch. Smart Angle found room on the outside and in a mighty effort gunned for Genuine Risk.

The fillies battled head and head through the stretch, and Smart Angle took the lead briefly at the eighth pole. Genuine Risk fought back, and the two swept under the wire, one lost in the silhouette of the other, with Genuine Risk putting her nose in front.

"At the eighth pole I thought I was beaten," LeRoy told *The Blood-Horse* after the race. "That's a good filly

of Woody's (Smart Angle's trainer Woody Stephens). I was happy to be second at that point."

LeRoy had to be happy with the effort, although he was not a man to show his pleasure outwardly. He was an intensely private person, a characteristic many members of the press mistook for rudeness. Not only had he won the race with Genuine Risk, but he also took show money with the good Big Spruce filly, Spruce Pine, whom he trained for longtime client John Greer.

Happiest of all were the Firestones, who knew they had an exceptional horse on their hands. "When she won the Demoiselle, beating divisional champion Smart Angle at mile and an eighth, we knew we had a super filly," Bert told *Daily Racing Form* in 1980.

Genuine Risk had banked $100,245 in her unbeaten season. She was ranked fifth among fillies on the 1979 Experimental Free Handicap at 116 pounds, behind Smart Angle, Table Hands, Royal Suite, and subsequent rival Bold 'n Determined. Smart Angle was declared champion two-year-old filly. It would be the last time that horsemen overlooked Genuine Risk as the top filly.

Derby Dreaming

G enuine Risk received a deserved break after her successful two-year-old season, wintering in Florida with the rest of LeRoy's stable.

Her first race at three came at Gulfstream Park on March 19 in a seven-furlong allowance for fillies. Carrying 113 pounds, Genuine Risk broke alertly under Jacinto. She won handily by two and a half lengths over Sober Jig and Peace Bells in a time of 1:22 3/5 on the fast track.

About this time Bert and Diana allowed themselves to think about the Kentucky Derby. The only filly to win the fabled race was Regret in 1915. No filly had even contested the Derby since 1959, when Silver Spoon ran into bad luck and finished fifth. It was now 1980 — could a filly actually win again?

Bert, Diana, and LeRoy began watching other

promising three-year-olds to evaluate Genuine Risk's chances. The filly still had a lot to prove before the team would devise a plan leading to Churchill Downs on the first Saturday in May.

After her victory at Gulfstream, Genuine Risk was shipped north to Aqueduct, site of three of her juvenile-season victories. A few weeks later, on April 5, LeRoy entered Genuine Risk in a mile handicap for fillies. Although the grade II Gotham Stakes was that day, the trainer stuck with the plan to race her against fillies one last time. LeRoy also entered John Greer's Spruce Pine, who had run a game third behind Genuine Risk in the Demoiselle.

This time Genuine Risk carried 124 pounds, her highest impost yet, and eleven pounds over her last start, but she paid no heed to the lead on her back. Midway through the race she pulled to the front and never looked back. She cruised to the winner's circle in 1:38 3/5, beating Tell a Secret by two and a quarter lengths. As in the Demoiselle, Spruce Pine ran third.

Genuine Risk's final time was more than two seconds slower than her time in the Tempted Stakes in November. Although the track was listed as good compared to fast for the Tempted, the time was slower than LeRoy would have liked. From a conditioning standpoint, the handicap had not accomplished what the trainer had hoped. "The race did nothing to put anything into her," he told *The Blood-Horse* after the race.

LeRoy knew that if Genuine Risk was going to face the colts in her next start, she needed a tune-up. He worked her at six furlongs in 1:13 2/5 a week after her tepid allowance victory. He began to wonder if he had pressed her too hard, too soon before her next race, but he didn't have much time to worry.

The grade I Wood Memorial at Aqueduct was just one week away, on April 19, and Genuine Risk would be there, taking on the colts with regular rider Jacinto Vasquez in the irons. LeRoy really wasn't keen on starting her against males, but according to the Wood Memorial report in *The Blood-Horse*, the Firestones wanted to run her. Jolley agreed, provided she didn't draw an outside post, but she received post position three and made the trip to the starting gate.

On a fast track Genuine Risk broke well for the mile and an eighth race. Running third, she set out in pursuit of leaders Plugged Nickle (of the misspelled

moniker) and Colonel Moran. Although she ran well, she remained in third the entire race, beaten only one and a half lengths despite having to alter course when Plugged Nickle drifted out. It was a game effort by the pretty chestnut filly.

After the race Jacinto lodged a foul against Plugged Nickle, claiming interference during the stretch run. The stewards disallowed the claim, and the results stood.

"Really, it was asking a tremendous amount of her to run in the Wood," LeRoy told *The Blood-Horse* later that year. "A lesser filly might have fallen apart. The Wood was an unusual race. Plugged Nickle and Colonel Moran went to the lead and they (with different owners, but the same trainer) must have been sort of friendly enemies. So there was no one to force the pace; Genuine Risk had to."

Shortly after the Wood, LeRoy told the media that Genuine Risk would not run in the Derby but instead would go to the Kentucky Oaks, the day before the Derby.

The Firestones were caught off guard by the announcement, which had not been discussed with them. They quickly set the record straight.

"We told him she had earned the right and was

going to run in the Derby," Bert recalled in 2003. "Eventually Jolley went along with our decision, but reluctantly."

LeRoy said he had decided on the Oaks after considering the potential of a few of the Derby nominees. In particular, Prince Valiant (by Stage Door Johnny) had impressed LeRoy with his performances in Florida in winning two allowance races, and in Louisiana capturing the grade II Louisiana Derby.

A few days later, Jolley began to reconsider, though not because of pressure from the Firestones. "Three or four days after the Wood, we galloped her and she just ran off with Jacinto," LeRoy said. "She really made the decision for everyone then."

The prestigious Blue Grass Stakes at Keeneland, traditionally the last big prep race for the Derby, clinched the decision when no colt emerged as a dominant force.

"The Blue Grass Stakes was the deciding part in the whole thing," LeRoy told *The Horsemen's Journal*. "We had been looking, trying to find a good colt. We looked and looked and looked. It was hard to find anything outstanding."

Jolley noted the Derby had always been a consider-

ation and that's why Genuine Risk had been nominated. "We pretty much saw all the races that had a bearing on the Derby," LeRoy said. "If Prince Valiant had won at Keeneland by a pole like he did at the Fair Grounds (in the Louisiana Derby), we might have stayed home." Prince Valiant finished last in the Blue Grass. The road to the Derby was over for him.

Bert felt good about the filly's chances. "A sense of history, or doing something different or sporting might have had something to do with our decision to run Genuine Risk in the Derby, but the main thing was, I thought we could win," Bert stated in *The Horsemen's Journal*.

The team moved on to Churchill Downs to fine-tune the filly. LeRoy was concerned about Genuine Risk's regaining her form after a tough race in the Wood. The Wednesday before the Derby, LeRoy sent her out with Jacinto to work five furlongs over a slow Churchill Downs surface. Her time for the workout was 1:02 2/5. LeRoy was not sure what to make of the time as it was slower than he wanted.

However, Jacinto reassured the trainer that Genuine Risk could handle the Derby despite the less-than-brilliant work. Jolley had confidence in the rider's opinion and relied on him for insight.

He told *The Blood-Horse*, "I felt better because of what Vasquez said after the work. His opinion is as good as any I've ever seen. (If he tells you a horse is no good, get rid of it.) He was a factor in deciding the filly would run in the Derby."

"Prior to the Derby, a lot of people talked about the slow workout," Jacinto recalled. "I wasn't worried though. I knew she didn't need a fast workout to be ready. And she was ready."

The stage was set for the filly to take on the colts on the first Saturday in May. Genuine Risk had a lot to prove to people who felt a filly was not worthy of taking on the colts.

As racing fans debated the filly's merits, breeder Sally Humphrey was following Genuine Risk's rise and path to the Kentucky Derby with loving interest. Suddenly Sally was being called for interviews and information about Genuine Risk's dam, Virtuous. Just two weeks before the Derby, Sally sold a half-interest in Virtuous to friend and horseman George Strawbridge Jr. Although George was pleased with his purchase, just two weeks later he would be ecstatic.

Despite Genuine Risk's obvious class, people doubted a filly could take the Derby. The last filly to try, C.V. Whitney's fine Silver Spoon, had finished fifth to Tomy Lee in 1959. Though the race had taken place more than twenty years earlier, racing fans had not forgotten the defeat. What they had forgotten, though, was the filly's subsequent victory over the Derby winner in the Cinema Handicap at Hollywood Park.

Genuine Risk's looks were deceiving, in that she was a very feminine filly with long eyelashes and a flashy chestnut coat. In a 1980 *Sports Illustrated* article, LeRoy commented that the filly was "more like Candice Bergen than Billie Jean King."

While bettors handicapped the field leading up to the race, the competitors went through workouts and prepared for the big day. The field presented an interesting dilemma for both casual and hardcore bettors. With the exception of Genuine Risk, no horse showed outstanding promise, but most bettors weren't willing to put their money on a filly.

According to *Time* magazine one bookmaker was heard to utter, "Any time a Derby field isn't strong enough to scare off the girls, you've got trouble."

The field for the 106th Derby included Bold 'n Rulling, Jaklin Klugman, Super Moment, Degenerate Jon, Rockhill Native, Gold Stage, Rumbo, Plugged Nickle, Withholding (who was just recovering from an injury), Execution's Reason, Tonka Wakhan, and Hazard Duke along with Genuine Risk. Just thirteen horses had found their way to Churchill Downs for the Run for the Roses, down from the 293 horses that had been nominated by the February 15 deadline.

Of the thirteen horses that made it to the starting gate, bettors set their sites on the previous year's champion juvenile male, Rockhill Native, trained by Derby newcomer Herb Stevens. Known to his crew as "Rocky," Rockhill Native had won the Blue Grass Stakes at Keeneland. The victory, his supporters said, signaled greater things to come.

Like Genuine Risk, Rockhill Native was a minority in the Derby due to being a gelding. Another entry, Execution's Reason, a 111-1 shot and a non-winner of four races leading up to the Derby, was also a gelding. Although geldings had contested the Derby on multiple occasions through the years, the last gelding to win was Clyde Van Dusen in 1929, and he was one of only

seven geldings to win the fabled race. Nevertheless, the track oddsmaker made Rockhill Native the favorite at 2.10-1.

Trainer T.J. Kelly's Plugged Nickle, winner of both the Wood Memorial and Florida Derby, came in as second choice at 2.60-1. Plugged Nickle might have been favored had he not breezed a weak mile in 1:41 3/5 on April 28.

Jaklin Klugman, a 7-1 shot trained by Riley Cofer, captured the California Derby on the way to Churchill Downs. Once at the track the colt won the mile Stepping Stone Purse, his first start outside of California. The gray colt attracted plenty of attention on the road to the roses because he was the namesake, in a way, and property of actor Jack Klugman, who owned him in partnership with John Dominguez. The colt had come by his feminine name when the owners mistakenly thought they were naming a filly.

The Ron McAnally-trained Super Moment, at Derby odds of 8-1, was owned by Maxwell Gluck's Elmendorf Farm. The late-running bay colt was still a mystery to many fans despite his second-place finish to Rockhill Native in the Blue Grass Stakes.

A more interesting prospect was the strong stretch-running Rumbo, at odds of 4-1 and trained by Thomas Bell Jr. Rumbo had finished second to Codex in both the Hollywood Derby and Santa Anita Derby. Laffit Pincay Jr. would be in the irons, but whether the skills of the veteran jockey could counteract the colt's well-known klutziness and propensity to spook remained to be seen. Known to shy at shadows, refuse to enter the starting gate, bump his head, and trip getting off airplanes, Rumbo seemed to be his own worst enemy.

The other horses were given long odds. Gold Stage was at 41-1; Bold 'n Rulling was 68-1; Degenerate Jon, 61-1; and Withholding, 64-1. Tonka Wakhan and Hazard Duke were coupled in the mutuel field and dismissed at 58-1.

Codex, the highly regarded California colt trained by D. Wayne Lukas, was ineligible for the race because he had not been nominated. At the time nominations were due, the late-developing Codex had only won two of ten races and hadn't stamped himself a Derby horse.

Several other good colts were going to miss the Derby. The winner of the Flamingo Stakes, Superbity, had bruised a foot. Koluctoo Bay, second to Superbity in that race, had suffered a slab fracture in the right knee.

As he viewed the field that had taken shape, LeRoy could only feel optimistic. Recently, thinking back on the time leading up to the race, LeRoy reflected, "(Genuine Risk) came up to the Derby very, very well. It always seemed just like fate. Everything went perfect for her, but didn't for the other horses."

He told *The Horsemen's Journal* after the Derby, "Everything improved her chances while the others seemed to have more difficulties the closer it got. They didn't train well, didn't look well when you saw them. Genuine Risk continued to blossom…"

CHAPTER 5

The Lady Is A Champ

Genuine Risk had more than long odds going against her in the Kentucky Derby. Sent off at 13.30-1 as the sixth betting choice, the filly would race one and a quarter miles for the first time in her career and also confront the strictures of history.

But what did she know of these limitations and challenges? Genuine Risk was primed to run the race of her life.

A crowd of 131,859 filled Churchill Downs on May 3, 1980, for the 106th Kentucky Derby. The day was clear, and by post time the temperature reached a comfortable 72 degrees, ensuring a fast track.

Many Derby patrons had also attended the races the day before when Saron Stable's Bold 'n Determined, Genuine Risk's future nemesis, galloped off with the Kentucky Oaks. Masterfully ridden by Eddie

Delahoussaye, Bold 'n Determined covered the one and one-sixteenth miles in 1:44 4/5.

The night before the Derby, Matt stayed up late reading the *Daily Racing Form*. He went to the barn the next morning with Bert and Diana to visit Genuine Risk. They also looked over the other contenders. Matt liked the look of Plugged Nickle but still thought Genuine Risk could beat the boys. And Bert showed confidence in his filly. He told William Nack of *Sports Illustrated*: "I wouldn't try for the Derby if I didn't think we had a good chance."

Matt and his parents gave their Derby morning interviews and headed to place bets for their friends. They then left the track to have brunch with Ed McGrath at his house. McGrath, a well-known Louisville insurance agent, hosted an annual Derby brunch.

By the afternoon the Firestone clan had reassembled at the track. They met in the paddock as Genuine Risk was saddled for the race. The large crowd made it difficult to get from the paddock to their box, and as they sat down, the horses were almost ready to go into the starting gate.

At 5:39 p.m. the field sprang from the gate. Genuine Risk broke well from post position ten. She settled into seventh place and held ground through the early backstretch. Approaching the half-mile pole, Jacinto decided to take her to the outside, and the filly moved up to fourth behind Bold 'n Rulling, Rockhill Native, and Plugged Nickle.

Though the pair had a problem-free trip, Jacinto heeded traffic on the front end. "I didn't want to go between horses and have pressure on the inside and outside; I thought that would cost me the race," he told the *New York Times*. "So I took back and tried to take advantage of things by going around."

As Genuine Risk's position improved, Rockhill Native lost his advantage when he ducked out at the three-quarters pole. Jockey John Oldham tried to regroup, but Rockhill Native didn't respond in his usual fashion at the top of the stretch.

Rockhill Native's untimely ducking out also compromised Plugged Nickle, according to his jockey, Buck Thornburg, a forty-seven-year-old grandfather who had hoped to become the oldest jockey to win the Derby.

Under the insistent left-handed whipping of Jacinto, Genuine Risk opened up by two lengths in the stretch. After trailing early, Rumbo made steady gains in the homestretch, but he could not catch the chestnut filly. Genuine Risk galloped away from the field and won by a length over the pursuing Rumbo in 2:02. The time was faster than either Seattle Slew (1977; 2:02 1/5) or Spectacular Bid (1979; 2:02 2/5) had run the race. Genuine Risk had accomplished what her maternal grandfather Gallant Man could not — a Derby victory.

Jaklin Klugman finished third, followed by Super Moment and the favorite Rockhill Native. Wood winner Plugged Nickle was seventh, just behind Bold 'n Rulling.

"When they turned the corner and hit the quarter pole, it hit you!" Matt said about Genuine Risk's stretch run. "It was crazy in the box. When she got in front, it felt like the wire would never get there. Time seemed to slow down. It seemed like a cavalry was chasing her, and we were hoping she was going to hang on."

Her victory was a affirmation for Matt, who had chosen her as a yearling. "It was amazing winning, having come close before," he recalled. "To finally win it with a horse most people didn't expect we could win it with was pretty exciting."

As LeRoy went to meet the winning pair, he was humbled by the rarity of his filly's accomplishment. He also acknowledged her great heart. "She gives everything for whatever you want her to do," he remembered thinking. Most of all he was truly happy for Genuine Risk, as she was perhaps the hardest-trying horse he had ever known.

Bert and Diana rushed down to the winner's circle. Six of their seven children ran after them. Diana was breathless and excited. "I knew it. I knew she could do it," she told *Sports Illustrated*.

"Everyone in our group started to move as soon as she crossed the finish line," Matt reminisced. "We had no time to hug, talk about the race, or watch Genuine Risk turn back toward the winner's circle. Our group ran out of the box — basically, it was a wild charge! The security tried to figure out who belonged in the group, and stopped Diana at one point. She had to push her way through.

"The next time I saw Genuine Risk, she was being led into the winner's circle. She was still blowing pret-

ty hard from the race, but boy, she looked great! She was also looking around very surprised to see so many people surrounding her."

Bert's assistant, Susan Grant, remembered the day as being a blur from all the excitement. "People were beside themselves with joy. We raced down, leapt over the fence, and toward the winner's circle. I look back on it now and wonder how I got over that fence."

Kentucky Governor John Brown and his wife Phyllis George, the former Miss America, joined the Firestones in the winner's circle. The governor proclaimed, "This is a woman's year."

Genuine Risk paid her believers $28.60, $10.60, and $4.80 on a two-dollar win ticket. She earned the Firestones a winner's purse of $250,550.

"We've had many thrills from racing over the years, but winning that Derby was the biggest thrill of our lives," Bert said in *Daily Racing Form*. "It's funny how racing is — we thought we'd win the Derby in 1976 with Honest Pleasure, but he finished second to Bold Forbes. Then we came back, a few years later, to win the Derby with a filly."

Despite LeRoy's initial misgivings about running

Genuine Risk in the Derby, the filly had proved the decision to be correct. "Am I pleased we came here? I am now. The filly went through a little low period there right after the Wood, and we all kept open minds about the Derby. I thought she'd run good in the Derby but I didn't think the race would be run that fast. I'm surprised, but not too much," he told the *New York Times*.

The always outspoken Angel Cordero also got in a word to the *Times*. "In my country (Puerto Rico), the fillies run against the colts all the time. If she can run, any filly can beat a colt. It's only in this country that they separate them, because they have so many good races for fillies. I thought she was the horse to beat all the time. She didn't surprise me at all, not after the race she ran the other day in the Wood. I don't think anybody had any excuse today. They're good colts, but they're not running any faster than they did before." Cordero had finished twelfth with Gold Stage.

Genuine Risk's victory had an impact on more than just her immediate connections. Her victory swayed racing fans such as Siobhan McGowan-DeLancey, who was convinced that Genuine Risk could not win the Derby. The filly taught her an important lesson.

"The year that Genuine Risk won the Derby, I conned my family into a friendly wagering system," Siobhan remembered. "We would each chip in a quarter and draw two names out of the field; the winner got the pot. I drew Genuine Risk and Degenerate Jon. Being a rather bratty eleven-year-old girl, I complained bitterly to my mother that Degenerate Jon was worthless, and that Genuine Risk had no chance. 'She's a filly!' I said in derision.

"Well, I guess I had to eat those words. My mother pointed out to me quietly after the race that girls could, in fact, do anything they chose — including beating the boys."

Along with Siobhan, many other horsemen and fans came to some new conclusions about the capabilities of fillies. Plugged Nickle's trainer T.J. Kelly stated in *The Blood-Horse*, "My hat's off to the ladies." But it was perhaps *Sports Illustrated* that said it best. The May 12 cover proclaimed "The Lady is a Champ."

GENUINE RISK

CHAPTER 6

They Don't Play This Game In Short Pants

After the Derby, cards and letters to the Firestones poured in from across the country. Bert and Diana even had to hire temporary help to assist with answering the thousands of notes Genuine Risk received. Each correspondent received a letter in return, along with an eight-by-ten photo of the filly.

Shortly after the Derby, Genuine Risk "sent" her dam, Virtuous, a dozen red roses for Mother's Day. No one now can remember who actually arranged the roses' delivery. The accompanying note from daughter to mother said in sum, "I couldn't have done it without you." Virtuous reportedly ate one of the roses upon receiving them.

"If she had been mine, the Kentucky Derby would have been her last race. I would have announced her retirement in the winner's circle and they'd still be writing songs and poems about her," trainer John Nerud told Russ Harris of the New York *Daily News* in 1981. But above all the Firestones were sportsmen. They felt they had the best three-year-old in the country and wanted to prove it.

Genuine Risk came into the 1980 Preakness strongly favored at 2-1 against her seven opponents, a field much smaller than the thirteen horses in the Derby.

Only one horse she had faced in the Derby tried his luck again, Jaklin Klugman. Jaklin Klugman's connections thought the slightly shorter one and three-sixteenths-mile distance of the Preakness would benefit their horse. Owners Jack Klugman and John Dominguez were also enjoying the ride through the Triple Crown, as the media spent a lot of time with the jovial actor Klugman.

Colonel Moran's connections also felt their horse had a good shot at the Preakness distance. He had finished second in the Wood, just behind Plugged Nickle but ahead of Genuine Risk. Jockey Jorge Velasquez would be in the irons for the Preakness.

Of the new challengers — Codex, Bing, Samoyed, Knight Landing, and Lucky Pluck — the West Coast-based Codex seemed most likely to give Genuine Risk a run for the money. He had won the Hollywood and Santa Anita derbys impressively and seemed to be a late-developing horse. Bettors thought he could bloom in Baltimore.

Codex was well-bred and striking looking. By Arts and Letters out of Roundup Rose, by Minnesota Mac, the dark chestnut colt was generating a loyal following. One mark against him, at least from a handicapping point of view, was the five weeks since his last race, the April 13 Hollywood Derby.

A big plus for Codex, however, was that jockey Angel Cordero Jr. would be in the saddle for the big race. Born in Santurce, Puerto Rico, in 1942, Angel grew up in the world of horse racing. His father, Angel Cordero Vila, was a trainer, and Angel Jr. followed him to the track. Since coming to the United States, Angel had posted a solid win record. Fans loved his aggressive style and huge smile.

But Angel could also be controversial. Leading up to the 1979 Belmont Stakes, Angel constantly baited young jockey Ronnie Franklin, who had ridden Spectacular Bid to Derby and Preakness victories.

Some people blamed Angel when Spectacular Bid lost the Belmont, and the Triple Crown, saying Cordero caused Franklin to unravel during the race.

Jockeys riding against Cordero sometimes had their work cut out for them. As LeRoy had once been famously quoted as saying about the sport, "They don't play this game in short pants." The upcoming Preakness would certainly be a haunting reminder of this racing adage.

On Preakness Day in 1980, a crowd of 83,455, the largest ever, turned out to see the 105th running. Most were there to see if their heroine, Genuine Risk, could beat the boys again. No filly had run in the race in forty-one years, and it had been fifty-six years since the filly Nellie Morse had come home in front.

When the gates sprung open, Genuine Risk broke in fifth place and then quickly dropped back to sixth. The 60-1 shot, Knight Landing, was leading, being pushed by Colonel Moran through the backstretch. At the half-mile pole Genuine Risk accelerated and pulled into fourth.

Coming into the final turn, Codex made a run for the lead on the inside. Genuine Risk matched his effort and hung tough on the outside.

Codex drifted very wide and brushed Genuine Risk, just as the filly was making her signature explosive move. At the same time, depending on whom you believe, Angel either hit Genuine Risk in the face with his whip or shook it in her face. The filly's charge was effectively stopped, and Codex rolled on to win easily in 1:54 1/5 on the fast track.

Genuine Risk was beaten by the largest margin of her career, four and three-quarters lengths. Unable to stay with the leaders, Colonel Moran finished third, another three and a quarter lengths back. Jaklin Klugman took fourth after making a stretch drive that fell short. The remaining order of finish was Bing, Samoyed, Knight Landing, and Lucky Pluck.

The crowd was shocked. Many booed and some stomped out of Pimlico, vowing never to return. Most felt Genuine Risk had been mugged. Everyone waited for the stewards to flash the inquiry sign, but the flashing light was not forthcoming. It took Jacinto's formal objection for the ten-minute inquiry to begin.

Jacinto was indignant and outraged. He defended Genuine Risk to anyone who would listen. In *Newsday* he was quoted as saying, "I thought this was a race-

track not a rodeo. I think they should have taken his (Codex's) number down. It is no different from any other race, no matter what the purse. It took the heart out of my filly when he brushed me. He sure brushed me hard. And Cordero hit my horse with his whip."

The *Lexington Herald-Leader* quoted Jacinto as saying, "He (Angel) hit my horse over the head. He did it on purpose. After that, she stopped running." The same article stated that Genuine Risk had gone back to the stable with a welt across her face from Cordero's whip.

In 2003 Jacinto still felt that Codex should have had his number taken down. "Those blind stewards should have disqualified Codex," he said. "Cordero probably could have beaten us fair and square. He didn't have to do that."

After some discussion the stewards allowed the finish to stand. If the majority of the crowd was upset before, now the fans were livid. Many claimed to have seen Cordero intentionally foul the filly by hitting her.

Longtime Turf writer Jim Hurley got a different glimpse of the fans' fury. "What I remember most about that day," Hurley recalled in the fall of 2002, "was rushing to the jocks' room after the race, and finding Cordero, tears streaming down his cheeks, on the phone talking to his then-wife Santa. After hanging up, he told me (there was not another reporter in sight) that Santa was receiving death threats. He asked me not to write about it. I agreed. At least until Monday when my story went back-page in the *New York Post*."

Members of the media also had strong opinions as to what had transpired. Hall of Fame jockey and ABC Sports commentator Eddie Arcaro weighed in on the issue. "I'm not a steward," he said to the *Baltimore Sun*, "but if I were, I'd have to take Codex's number down."

William Boniface, the *Baltimore Evening Sun* racing editor, did not mince words. "In an ungentlemanly display of poor manners, Codex, a big chestnut colt from the West Coast, defeated the popular filly Genuine Risk…The soundness of the decision not to disqualify Codex, who paid $7.40, $3.60, and $3.80, will be debated far beyond next year's Preakness."

Writer Phil Jackman of the *Baltimore Sun* asked, "When is a foul not a foul? A couple of times: 1) When an official doesn't see it, and 2) when committed at a Maryland track during the feature race on the third Saturday in May."

In *Newsday*, Angel defended his riding. "My horse

was way on the outside before the filly got to him. I was already there. There was no contact. And I didn't hit him with my whip. When the filly came up to us my horse took off again.

"If I had been second I would have claimed (foul). Everybody takes a shot in a big race. It's another chance to win, a part of the game. But I don't think I carried him [Genuine Risk] out, and there was no contact, no nothing. If I do anything, my number would have come down."

If the crowd was angry and shocked, Genuine Risk's connections were more so. Sally Humphrey and her husband, Watts, "didn't have the best seats at the Preakness," remembered the filly's breeder. "I couldn't see a thing. Watts ended up climbing up a pole to see the race. I didn't get to see the race, even though I was there, until that night on the news. We were very upset by what happened to Genuine Risk."

Sally was frustrated that the stewards did not take down Codex's number, and she was angry with Angel for the way he rode.

Exercise rider and assistant trainer John Nazareth was furious. He felt the stewards hadn't done their job.

He told Maryjean Wall of the *Lexington Herald-Leader*, "One was blind, one was deaf, and one must have been drinking too many daisies," a reference to the official drink of the Preakness, the Black-Eyed Susan.

John also spoke with Bill Tanton of the *Baltimore Sun*. "Cordero looked back and saw our horse, and then he hit her with his whip. Twenty million people saw it. Suppose he had hit her in the eye instead of on her head? These stewards should be fired. If I made a mistake like that in my job, I'd be gone. LeRoy worked hard to get her to her peak for this. We had her right on ready, and then something like this happens. It's horrible."

"They did brush or bump," LeRoy told the *Baltimore Sun* after the race. He was deeply disappointed but surprisingly calm as he spoke to the press. "But Codex continued well after that, and we didn't continue so well. I'm not crazy about the stewards decision. I thought their (Codex's) number would come down. But there seem to be two different worlds — one for the competitors and the other for the officials." In the Preakness barn LeRoy made a point to walk down and congratulate the winning trainer, D. Wayne Lukas.

LeRoy recently stated, "I still haven't changed my

mind one bit after all these years, and I doubt serious-
ly anyone who has seen the race has changed their
mind. Had it been any other race but a Triple Crown
race, Codex's number would have come down. No
horse up to that time that had finished first or second
had been disqualified in a Triple Crown race, and I
think that weighed heavily on the stewards."

Although a winner had never been knocked down
for a foul infraction in the Preakness, Pimlico stewards
had taken action twelve years before with a third-place
finisher, a horse that already had a black mark on his
name. In the 1968 Preakness, Dancer's Image, who
had made headlines just days before as the first
Kentucky Derby winner to be disqualified in a drug-
related offense, was disqualified by the stewards and
placed eighth for bumping Martins Jig, who had ended
up eighth. According to the *Daily Racing Form* chart,
Dancer's Image had "bullied his way through" a nar-
row opening at the furlong pole.

Some racing people felt that the 1968 Dancer's Image
foul of Martins Jig was a far less serious infraction than
what happened between Codex and Genuine Risk.
Apparently, the stewards didn't see it the same way.

Although the finish of the Preakness was a disappointment to the Genuine Risk team, the filly returned to the barn sound, albeit roughed up. "She tried so hard; every race took a lot out of her because she tried so hard. The Preakness certainly took something out of her; there's no doubt about that," LeRoy said.

After the Preakness, a batch of letters from a group of schoolchildren went to the Firestone Tire Company (no relation to Bert and Diana) instead of the Firestone family. The tire company forwarded the notes on to Bert and Diana. Bert's assistant Susan Grant remembered opening the package.

"All these children had drawn pictures of Genuine Risk. Some of the drawings were just of Genuine Risk; others showed Codex and Genuine Risk together, with the filly being hit in the face with a whip. A lot of the pictures had very heartfelt notes on them and others said things like 'she was robbed.' Some even said that Codex was an evil horse for winning the Preakness. It was amazing how many people cared passionately about the outcome of that race."

Right after the Preakness the Firestones issued a statement that read "While Genuine Risk was in the

midst of her critical stretch drive to pass Codex, she was bumped and pushed wide by Codex and was hit on the head by Cordero's whip. We don't know the intentions of Codex's jockey, but we are sorry this incident prevented the fair race to the finish line. We are very happy that Genuine Risk did not sustain a serious injury. We, of course, accept the result of this race, and would like to congratulate the winner."

Not long after this gracious statement was issued, however, Bert and Diana decided to appeal the stewards' decision.

CHAPTER 7

The Appeal

F ans were almost universal in their support of Genuine Risk and in their condemnation of Angel Cordero. Hundreds of letters from all over the country deluged the *Baltimore Sun*. The missives were critical of the stewards' failure to take action. Headlines from the letters screamed "Bad deal," "Ban Cordero," "Fans cheated," "Gutless," "Risk robbed," and "Justice foiled."

G.A. Wickstrom of Newell, West Virginia, wrote regarding the competency of the stewards. "…I am positive that the stable boys could have done much better. The stewards at Pimlico ought to be relegated to the task of mucking stalls."

Although Pimlico stewards Fred Colwill, Clinton Pitts Jr., and Eddie Litzenberger, who all were former riders, had hoped the issue would go away, the furor grew. Soon, everything from the stewards' qualifications to

Pimlico's videotaping system was being questioned.

Codex's trainer, D. Wayne Lukas, was just as unhappy as everyone else. He felt his horse had run a good race and wasn't being recognized for his efforts. "I wish the race had been cleanly run," he told the *Baltimore Sun*. "I wish there had been no controversy. I wish America was waking up hailing Codex for his victory. Instead, I get a telegram from a woman in Miami telling me I'm just a lousy, Quarter Horse bum."

On May 19, just a couple of days after the Preakness, the Firestones appealed to the Maryland Racing Commission's Thoroughbred Board to review the stewards' decision. The couple explained their decision in a press release saying, "After considerable thought and discussion with horsemen throughout the country, we have decided to appeal to the Maryland Racing Commission the decision of the stewards at Pimlico Race Course disallowing the objection of our jockey, Jacinto Vasquez, in the Preakness Stakes on Saturday.

"We feel that the interests of the racing public and Genuine Risk would be well served by having the matter reviewed in the manner provided for under the Maryland racing rules. Should the appeal be allowed, the entire purse will be donated to the National Museum of Racing and to furthering the interest of equine research."

In the meantime purse distribution for the race was held up.

On June 2 the Maryland Racing Commission met at Pimlico to discuss the appeal. Although there were five board members, only four heard the case. Bob Furtick, an eleven-year veteran of the board, disqualified himself from the hearing after some sources reported he had commented "hooray" when he heard the Firestones would be appealing. He had also been quoted in the media that he felt that Genuine Risk's number should have been put up.

The remaining board members hearing the case were fairly new on the job, and some in the media questioned their qualifications. Robert Banning, the chairman, had only served since 1977, the same year Frank Cuccia started. Both had been car dealers. Neil McCardell, who ran an office supply company, joined them in 1978. The final member, retired circuit court judge Kenneth Proctor, began serving in 1979.

The hearing lasted three days. Attorney Henry Lord

represented the Firestones, while Arnold Weiner acted on behalf of Codex's owner, Tartan Farms.

Coleman "Coley" Blind, the son of longtime starter Eddie Blind, had a statement read to the board. Blind was the patrol judge at the quarter pole and was nearest the incident in question. He notified the stewards during the race that Codex was carrying Genuine Risk wide. This was verified on the transcript of the stewards' audiotape of the race, which contained the track announcer's call and the patrol judges' comments.

The written transcript of the stewards' tape made for interesting reading. The voice of Coley Blind was heard telling the stewards "...Oh, three's carrying five wide on the turn, Judge! (pause) Stewards?"

A steward responded, "Yeah." Blind then said, "Turning for home, Cordero looked back just prior to the quarter pole, knew she was coming on the outside and carried her wide."

One steward replied, "All right," and another said, "He took her out," while yet another voice said, "Huh?"

Two days after the race Blind was sure of what he had seen, and detailed it in writing, according to a report in the *Sun*.

The chief steward, Fred Colwill, wasn't happy with a patrol judge telling him how to do his job. He disagreed with Blind, saying, "I'd rather make up my own mind than have Coley Blind tell me," the *Sun* reported.

One of the points of contention was what the stewards were seeing on the videotape. Many people contended that Pimlico's system was inadequate and that the ABC Sports tapes gave a clearer view of the alleged incident. The ABC tapes were in color, allowed a much closer view of the action, and included slow motion and an isolated camera view of Genuine Risk. The stewards' videotapes had none of these capabilities.

The board heard testimony from many of the people involved. Both Vasquez and Cordero reiterated their differing views of the race. According to the *Baltimore Sun*, Vasquez forcefully said, "He (Angel) knocked my filly off her stride and I had to hold on with all my might to get her to turn. My filly was struck with the whip at least once."

Cordero denied any wrongdoing but did allow that his horse had drifted out a little.

D. Wayne Lukas told the board that his instructions to Cordero before the race had included the directive to

ride Codex to the outside. Jolley stated once again that Genuine Risk was bumped, carried wide, and hit with Cordero's whip.

The Firestones brought in Hall of Fame jockey Ted Atkinson, a retired steward, to testify. In his statement Atkinson said that Codex's number should have come down because the colt had carried the filly wide. He also pointed out that that Cordero's whip must have hit Genuine Risk.

The ABC Sports tapes were viewed. Television photographer Fred Eichenberg testified that ABC Sports' camera angles could not provide an accurate picture of what had transpired. This was despite the fact that most casual racing fans felt they had seen "proof" of an infraction on the ABC telecast.

The race, like others, was videotaped by the Pimlico staff from five angles, all of which were scrutinized. Many people felt that the closed-circuit views the stewards watched at Pimlico were insufficient to determine what had happened. The tapes were decidedly unclear, although steward Colwill felt they were fine. Jolley stated tracks in other states had superior videotape capabilities compared with Pimlico's.

The board and the lawyers scrutinized twenty-six photos taken by Weyman Swagger, a photographer from the *Baltimore Sun*. The board hoped to find another view of the incident in the photos, but what the photos revealed, or didn't reveal, was debated.

The board also interviewed jockey Bill Passmore, the rider of early-running Knight Landing. He had been behind both Genuine Risk and Codex when the incident occurred and testified, "it looked like Codex carried Genuine Risk very wide — about six horse widths — and should have been disqualified. But, since the stewards' decision has been made, I believe it should remain. Someone has to be in charge at the track and that's the responsibility of the stewards. Once they make a judgment call, I will abide by it."

At the time of the 1980 Preakness, Passmore had been the leading rider in Maryland for two years. Ironically, Passmore is now a Maryland steward.

In December 2002 he told the *Mid-Atlantic Thoroughbred* in an article about the 1980 Preakness, "I had a ringside seat. I got subpoenaed. I testified before the commission. They asked me my opinion. In my opinion Codex's number would come down. That was

my opinion. But I also testified that it was a judgment call and that the number should stand."

Bert was the final witness called by Henry Lord at the appeal. He was strident in his statement. "I think it is a disgrace to Maryland racing and racing in general when Codex was not disqualified after 30 million people had seen it (the alleged foul) happen on television."

At the end of the hearing, the board voted three-to-one to back the stewards and uphold the finish of the race. Neil McCardell was the dissenter. He wanted Cordero to be suspended and fined and Codex to be disqualified.

Genuine Risk's team was disappointed, but realized that further fighting was futile. They knew that it would be a rare event for the board to overturn the stewards' original decision. Historically, the board almost always backed the stewards.

Although Bert and Diana had discussed civil litigation, they decided against it. They issued a statement, which read in part, "We have decided not to carry this matter to the courts. It is difficult to overturn a steward's decision — even an obviously incorrect one. We feel sure Genuine Risk would have won the Preakness had she not been impeded during her critical stretch run.

"We are also pleased to offer fans of racing a horse who gives her best running on just oats, hay, and water." This comment was a direct swipe at Codex, who had contested the Preakness while running on Lasix and Bute.

In the October 1980 issue of *The Horsemen's Journal*, Bert commented on the hearing. "There was no way they (the commission) were going to change the decision. I personally don't believe in overturning stewards. I think when you hire stewards they should be very competent people. I also believe every race is the same, whether it's a claiming race, an allowance race or a stakes race. When you break the rules in a claiming race, they should take the number down. When you break the rules in an allowance race, they should take the number down. The same thing holds when you break the rules in the classic races. They should take the number down. But the Pimlico stewards felt that this was a classic race, and no one's ever done it before, and that's why they didn't take the number down, in my opinion."

Bert and Diana both felt that the public and anyone

who had listened to the hearing knew that Genuine Risk was the true winner of the race. Bert said he had no regrets about appealing and would do it all over again.

Matt spoke about the race during the winter of 2003. "A year or so ago, I found a tape of the race and re-watched it. I've seen horses taken down today for a lot less of an infraction. I've been on both sides of the issue. Any other race, any other day, she would have been put up (to first)."

Not much has changed in the minds of Bert and Diana over the years. In 2003 they stated, "We felt Genuine Risk definitely would have won the race had she not been bothered by the other horse and rider. There had never been a DQ in the classic races before, and the stewards were probably hesitant about taking a number down. The other horse's number should have come down."

Even though Genuine Risk's team was disappointed in the wake of the Preakness, there was one more Triple Crown race to get ready for. The team would move on to Belmont to try to avenge the filly's defeat.

CHAPTER 8

Dancing Every Dance

The Wednesday prior to the Belmont Genuine Risk blazed five-eighths of a mile in 1:00 4/5. What made the workout even more impressive was that Jacinto really only let her run for about an eighth of a mile. Backstretch workers sat up and took notice, but many members of the media had already jumped ship and were backing Codex.

LeRoy was pleased with the filly's Belmont preparations. He told the *Baltimore Sun* that the work was "terrific, just terrific, but more than that she looks and acts better than she ever has and that's with three hard races behind her."

The tension simmering between Jacinto and Angel followed them to New York. Jacinto in particular was still carrying a grudge from the Preakness incident. Losing the appeal did not help.

He told Dale Austin of the *Baltimore Sun*, "If Angel pulls the same kind of stunt in the Belmont that he pulled in the Preakness, I won't leave it up to the stewards to make the decision. I'll make my own decision, and you will see those two horses come back without riders."

After the Preakness, Jacinto had told the press the race had been like a rodeo, so when Angel heard Jacinto's comment about the riderless horses, he had a quick rejoinder: "I'll be wearing my cowboy hat and carrying my lasso, so I'll be okay."

To add to the drama, the post position draw put Genuine Risk and Codex side by side for the start of the mile and a half race, in the first and second post positions, respectively. Angel took this in stride. "I just hope they don't fall in love at the gate. If they ever get married, they ought to name the foal Controversy."

Despite Angel's light tone the Belmont stewards knew that the situation between Angel and Jacinto could explode into something more serious. Both riders were called in for a conference with stewards John Rotz, Gerry Burke, and Sal Ferrara. Burke, speaking on behalf of the stewards, said after the conference, "We cautioned them both in strong terms that we expect all riders to maintain the integrity of the Belmont Stakes."

Ten horses were entered for the final leg of the Triple Crown. Codex was favored at 1.60-1 while Genuine Risk was relegated to third choice at 5-1 behind her Derby runner-up Rumbo, at 5-2.

Derby starters Super Moment and Rockhill Native, the latter having bypassed the Preakness due to a knee injury, returned for a try at the final American classic. Both received lukewarm attention, with Rockhill Native at 12.80-1 and Super Moment at 13-1. Preakness fifth-place finisher Bing also returned but was dismissed as the longest shot in the race at 119-1.

Four horses — Pikotazo, Comptroller, Joanie's Chief, and Temperence Hill — were newcomers to the Triple Crown scene. Perhaps the most interesting was Pikotazo, a horse from Mexico with a nine-race winning streak, including the Derby Mexicano. His owner, Gustavo Zepeda Carranza, spent more than $30,000, between the $20,000 supplement fee and shipping, to bring Pikotazo to the Belmont to take on the American horses. Handicappers didn't completely discount his chances, making him the fourth choice at 8-1.

Ogden Phipps' Comptroller, a 26-1 shot, had galloped to victory in the grade III Peter Pan Stakes at Belmont Park a little over a week before, and his connections were optimistic that the colt might be able to handle the Belmont distance. The Eugene Jacobs-trained Joanie's Chief, the second-longest shot at 101-1, had won the grade I Champagne Stakes as a two-year-old but hadn't won a race since.

Temperence Hill was another longshot at 53-1. Trainer Joe Cantey, husband of television personality and exercise rider Charlsie Cantey, had brought in the Arkansas Derby winner to take on the field. Jockey Eddie Maple got the call to ride the son of Stop the Music for owner John Ed Anthony of Loblolly Stable.

Anthony had to supplement Temperence Hill for $20,000 to the Belmont. At the time Kentucky Derby nominations were due in February, Temperence Hill had not won a race. Within months, however, the late-developing colt galloped home to win the Rebel Handicap and Arkansas Derby and finish second in the mile Withers, a race sandwiched between Genuine Risk's Derby and Codex's Preakness.

But a resounding defeat in the Pennsylvania Derby just nine day after the Preakness had left questions about whether the Belmont should be added to Temperence Hill's schedule. Anthony and Cantey wanted one more race prior to the Belmont to help them make up their minds. On May 31, just seven days before the Belmont Stakes, Temperence Hill faced older horses in a mile and one-sixteenth allowance on the Belmont turf. Although he did not win, the big horse put in a good run and finished third. With that finish, Temperence Hill earned a chance at the big race.

Although Codex could not run on Bute and Lasix in New York due to the state's strict medication rules, his status as favorite was not affected. His trainer, D. Wayne Lukas, had never run the colt without medication, but said he was sure the horse would run just as well. "The use of Butazolidin and Lasix is permitted in California and I run all my horses on it. I know this colt and have no reason to think he'll run differently without medication in the Belmont. He's completely sound of limb and I'm confident he'll run a top race," Lukas told writer William Boniface of the *Baltimore Evening Sun*.

Race day dawned rainy and damp, assuring a muddy track for the Belmont Stakes. Trainers wrestled with whether to use horseshoes with mud caulks.

Everyone decided against it except Joe Cantey, who put the cleated shoes on Temperence Hill.

When the horses entered the paddock to be saddled, it was clear from the cheers that Genuine Risk was the sentimental favorite, even if she wasn't the betting favorite. The New York fans voraciously booed Angel Cordero, who shrugged it off.

As in the Derby and Preakness, the filly was carrying 121 pounds, five pounds less than the colts.

At the start the filly broke well and dropped back to race inside around the first turn. Comptroller moved into the lead heading into the backstretch, closely followed by Pikotazo, Codex, and Bing. Rockhill Native made a run at the leaders on the outside around the first turn and took the lead through the backstretch.

Jacinto recognized that the pace was slow (the fractions were :24 3/5, :50 1/5, 1:15 1/5, 1:39 3/5) and that if he didn't do something, Rockhill Native might run off with the race. He sent Genuine Risk out after Rockhill Native and Codex. Eddie Maple realized the same thing, and he pushed along Temperence Hill.

Into the stretch Genuine Risk made a run for it with Rockhill Native on her inside and Temperence Hill on the outside. Rumbo made a late charge but was unable to catch the leaders.

Genuine Risk reached deep inside and put her nose in front at midstretch, but she couldn't hang on. In the last sixteenth of a mile, Temperence Hill drew away to finish ahead of the filly by two lengths in time of 2:29 4/5. He paid a whopping $108.80 for the win.

Genuine Risk finished second, one and a half lengths in front of Rockhill Native. Comptroller hung on for fourth, with Rumbo fifth.

The favorite, Codex, had dropped from contention on the final turn. The official chart declared that Codex was "finished after going nine furlongs." Afterward, race fans debated whether he tired because of the distance or because he lacked his usual medications.

"Genuine Risk ran a tremendous race in the Belmont," LeRoy recalled. "She tried her heart out. You also have to remember that the horse that beat her, Temperence Hill, became that year's champion three-year-old. He loved mud and was a late developer."

Bert was proud of his filly. "She ran a beautiful race and finished second. Codex finished toward the back of the field."

Matt had accompanied his parents to the Belmont and remembered that day well. "She tried as hard as she could against the colts," he said. But there might have been a reason for her loss. "She spiked a fever a day or two after the race, and there might have been something going on when she raced. It's hard to tell with those things."

The Belmont would be Rockhill Native's final start. He retired with a total of ten wins, two seconds, and three thirds out of seventeen starts and earnings of $465,122. In each of their races together, Rockhill Native's game style had pushed Genuine Risk to excel.

The Belmont was also Codex's last start. In mid-October the colt was retired and syndicated for stud duty at Tartan near Ocala, Florida. His record: six wins in fifteen starts and earnings of $534,576.

When all was said and done, Genuine Risk had accomplished what no other filly had ever done. She had raced in each leg of the Triple Crown and never finished lower than second. Genuine Risk had danced every dance.

CHAPTER 9

A Meeting Of Titans

The rigors of the Triple Crown had taken their toll, and after the Belmont, Genuine Risk ended up getting a three-month break even though that wasn't necessarily the plan. She did not train well in the summer heat in New York. LeRoy had wanted to enter the filly in either the Alabama or Travers Stakes at Saratoga but chose to give her some time off instead.

LeRoy decided to bring back Genuine Risk against the girls at Belmont in the grade II Maskette Stakes on September 10. Long-range plans called for her to run in the Ruffian and Beldame, both grade I, at Belmont, and then move to Keeneland to finish her season in the grade I Spinster Stakes.

A group of outstanding fillies and mares made up the field for what would be an historic running of the Maskette. Genuine Risk would meet two winners of the Kentucky Oaks, Davona Dale (1979) and Bold 'n Determined (1980). Genuine Risk had not raced for more than thirteen weeks, while Bold 'n Determined was coming off a ten-week layoff. Love Sign, the grade II Gazelle Handicap winner, and Croquis, the grade I Delaware Handicap runner-up, were also among the contenders.

More than one racing writer had bemoaned the lack of depth in the field of colts in 1980. This was certainly not the case with the fillies and mares, who provided the biggest thrills of the year. Of all the girls, six stood out: Genuine Risk, Davona Dale, Bold 'n Determined, Love Sign, Misty Gallore, and It's in the Air. Four of the six would meet in the Maskette. Three would meet in the Ruffian Handicap.

Calumet Farm's Davona Dale (by Best Turn out of Royal Entrance, by Tim Tam) was trained by John Veitch, who had helped Calumet Farm regain some of its lost luster with 1977 three-year-old filly champion Our Mims and with her half brother Alydar, who ran second in all of the 1978 Triple Crown races.

Davona Dale had never finished worse than fourth. In 1979 she had won races all over the country, including the Debutante Stakes at Fair Grounds, the Fantasy Stakes at Oaklawn Park, the Kentucky Oaks at Churchill Downs, and the Black-Eyed Susan Stakes at Pimlico. She also had taken all three legs of the New York Filly Triple Crown (now known as the Triple Tiara). The filly lost the Alabama to It's in the Air one week prior to facing the boys in the Travers and finished fourth to General Assembly in the latter race. She finished her 1979 season with a fourth in the Maskette Stakes and earned champion three-year-old filly honors.

During the summer of 1980, she won the grade III Ballerina Stakes at Saratoga. Veitch then pointed Davona Dale again at the Maskette.

The Neil Drysdale-trained Bold 'n Determined (by Bold and Brave out of Pidi, by Determine) had won the 1980 Kentucky Oaks, Acorn Stakes, and Coaching Club American Oaks. She had just missed winning the Mother Goose by a head to Calumet Farm's Sugar and Spice.

Genuine Risk and Davona Dale went to the post in the Maskette as co-favorites at 6-5 odds. Under the handicap conditions of the race, Genuine Risk was carrying 118 pounds while the older Davona Dale was sad-

dled with 123 pounds. Bold 'n Determined carried 122 pounds and was sent off at odds of 10-1. Love Sign was assigned 120 pounds. Croquis carried only 114 pounds as she was a non-winner of four races that season.

Love Sign broke on top in the mile race and soon led by nearly three lengths. She was followed by Bold 'n Determined, then Davona Dale, and Genuine Risk, five lengths back. The quarter came in :23 2/5, while the half rang in at :46 1/5, moderate times on a fast track.

After three-quarters in 1:10 4/5, Bold 'n Determined and Davona Dale made a move on Love Sign and pulled up to her. Genuine Risk was running right behind Davona Dale and got ready to unleash her characteristic late charge.

Jacinto was having problems reading the horses in front of him. He was hoping for a spot to open on the rail if Love Sign faded but decided he couldn't take the chance. He swung outside of Davona Dale, and Genuine Risk plunged forward. At the top of the stretch, Genuine Risk had moved into the lead.

Davona Dale had run out of steam, but Bold 'n Determined put in a late charge and went after the leader. At the eighth pole Genuine Risk and Bold 'n

Determined raced as one. But by the sixteenth pole
Bold 'n Determined had moved ahead by a half-length.

Then, Genuine Risk did something that no one had
seen her do before — she began to come back on the
leader. She was showing she wasn't just a one-run filly.
Genuine Risk ground down Bold 'n Determined's lead and
would not give up. But at the wire, Bold 'n Determined
stubbornly stuck her nose in front of Genuine Risk, leaving the Firestone filly with second place. Love Sign finished third, while champion Davona Dale finished fourth
yet again in the Maskette. It was Davona Dale's last race.
She was headed to the breeding shed.

Although Genuine Risk had lost by mere inches, it
was a valiant effort coming off so long a layoff. The fans
were anxious to see another meeting between Bold 'n
Determined and Genuine Risk. Many felt the three
year-old filly championship honors hung in the bal-
ance between these two warriors.

LeRoy kept Genuine Risk on track for the Ruffian
Handicap just seventeen days later on September 27 at
Belmont. Neil Drysdale opted to run Bold 'n
Determined in an allowance race at Keeneland to prep
for the Spinster Stakes.

Genuine Risk captured the hearts of racing fans everywhere when she boldly took on the boys in the Kentucky Derby and won.

Genuine Risk was sired by Exclusive Native (above), who also sired 1978 Triple Crown winner Affirmed. Exclusive Native's sire, Raise a Native (left), was a brilliant two-year-old who established himself as a top sire and sire of sires. Virtuous (below left), the dam of Genuine Risk, was a winning daughter of 1957 Belmont Stakes winner Gallant Man (below).

Genuine Risk was the first horse bred by Sally Humphrey (top, far right). Sally and her husband, G. Watts Humphrey (third from left), own Shawnee Farm in Kentucky. In the barn shown above, a nameplate marks the stall in which Genuine Risk was foaled. Champions Sacahuista, Bornastar, and Misil were born in the same stall.

GENUINE RISK
EXCLUSIVE NATIVE   -   VIRTUOUS

Matthew Firestone (inset, right) picked Genuine Risk out at auction when he was only fourteen years old. Bert and Diana Firestone (above with daughter Alison) raced the chestnut filly, who blossomed under the care of trainer LeRoy Jolley (below with his stable star). Jacinto Vasquez, who rode numerous greats in the 1970s, added Genuine Risk to his impressive resume.

Genuine Risk raced in Diana Firestone's name. Diana looked on as her filly visited the Belmont winner's circle after her first start (above). After a subsequent allowance win, Genuine Risk added victories in the Tempted Stakes (below) and Demoiselle (left) to go four-for-four at two.

After a couple of easy allowance victories, Genuine Risk was sent against the boys for the first time in the Wood Memorial (below), in which she finished a tough third. Her game effort and a lack of strong contenders among the colts convinced her connections to try her in the Kentucky Derby and off she went to Churchill Downs (above).

After taking the lead entering the stretch, Genuine Risk put away favored Rockhill Native and the grey Jaklin Klugman (top) and resolutely held off a late-closing Rumbo for the victory (above). In winning, Genuine Risk (right in the winner's circle) became the first female Kentucky Derby winner since Regret in 1915.

Genuine Risk was sent to Pimlico to prepare for the Preakness (right). It had been forty-one years since a filly had contested the Preakness, and Genuine Risk seemed poised to make another winning move when she was carried wide by Codex (top) coming out of the final turn. Codex went on to win with Genuine Risk holding on for second (above). The Firestones filed an appeal to have Codex disqualified for the alleged "mugging," but the Maryland Racing Commission let the finish stand. Genuine Risk went on to the Belmont Stakes (opposite, top) and finished a game second in the mud (opposite) to earn the best record for a filly in all three Triple Crown races. She was already a champion to her fans.

THE LADY IS
A CHAMP
GENUINE RISK

Genuine Risk returned after a three-month break to face another tough challenger: Bold 'n Determined in the Maskette Stakes. Bold 'n Determined, who had won the Kentucky Oaks, held off Genuine Risk by just a nose (above). Genuine Risk finished her three-year-old season with another nailbiter in the Ruffian Handicap, winning by a nose over Misty Gallore.

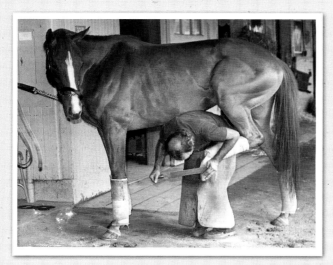

Named champion three-year-old filly for her Triple Crown heroics, Genuine Risk kept to her routine as she prepared for her four-year-old debut.

Genuine Risk blazed home by nine and a half lengths in allowance company for her first start at four (top). She then worked on grass (above) at Belmont to prep for her second start, a grass allowance, in which she finished third. The chestnut filly made what was her final start at Saratoga (left), easily taking a seven-furlong allowance. A freak accident at Belmont Park led to her premature retirement.

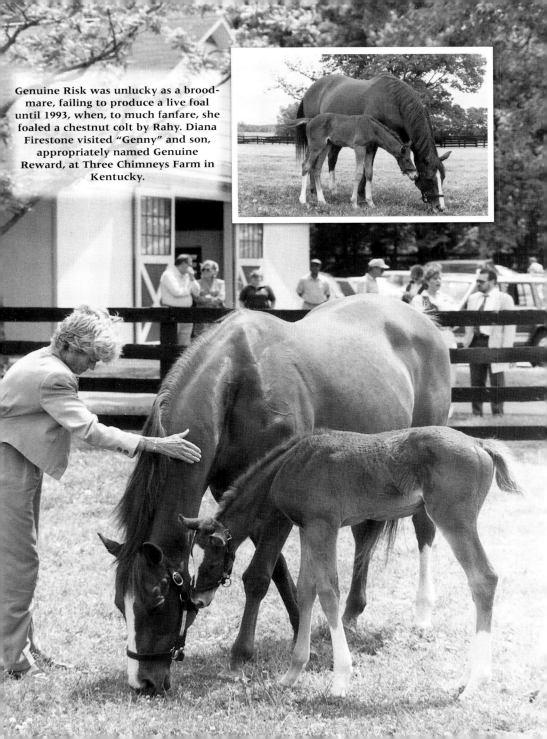

Genuine Risk was unlucky as a brood-mare, failing to produce a live foal until 1993, when, to much fanfare, she foaled a chestnut colt by Rahy. Diana Firestone visited "Genny" and son, appropriately named Genuine Reward, at Three Chimneys Farm in Kentucky.

Before being pensioned, Genuine Risk produced one more foal, another flashy chestnut colt (above). Named Count Our Blessing, the colt (left at Laurel Park) was by the Firestone's grade I-winning home-bred stallion Chief Honcho. Unfortunately, neither Genuine Reward nor Count Our Blessing ever raced.

Genuine Risk was pensioned in 2000 and sent to the Firestones' Newstead Farm in Virginia to live a quiet, dignified life deserving of a champion.

The Kentucky Derby-winning fillies: Genuine Risk (1980; above), Regret (1915; left), and Winning Colors (1988; below).

A fast track awaited Genuine Risk for the Ruffian. She faced only five opponents — the hard-knocking Misty Gallore, It's in the Air, Love You Dear, Heavenly Ade, and Blitey — for the mile and one-eighth race. Genuine Risk and It's in the Air both carried 118 pounds while the older Misty Gallore was under 124 pounds. The Ruffian came down to those three.

It's in the Air led heading down the backstretch, with Misty Gallore right behind her.

Genuine Risk, who broke from the inside post position, pulled in behind the leaders. By the top of the stretch, Genuine Risk found room to run on the rail. The three fillies matched each other stride for stride across the track, straining for the finish line. Genuine Risk held on by a nose, followed by Misty Gallore, who was a neck in front of It's in the Air.

"I honestly didn't know who won," said LeRoy after the close race. "I had to wait like everyone else to see the numbers go up."

Don MacBeth had piloted Misty Gallore, and Jeff Fell was in the irons aboard It's in the Air. Both MacBeth and Fell got to see Genuine Risk at her toughest. That knowledge would help them later when each rode her in a race.

After the Ruffian Handicap, Genuine Risk came back to the barn in fine fettle. LeRoy continued training her toward the Beldame Stakes, and all was going smoothly until the day of the race.

On October 11, the morning of the Beldame, Genuine Risk walked out of the barn, lame in her left front foot. LeRoy immediately scratched her from the race and then went about finding out what was wrong. An infection was cut out of her hoof, but that was the least of her problems. An X-ray showed a chip in her left knee, although LeRoy wasn't sure when it could have happened. "She had been walking and galloping fine through yesterday," he told reporters at his barn. The trainer didn't discount the unhappy possibility of retiring Genuine Risk.

But Bert and Diana didn't want to give up on racing Genuine Risk just yet. The Firestones and LeRoy jointly decided to give her the rest of the year off and see how she faired. They shipped her to the farm in Virginia for a respite from work and sent her to Miami, LeRoy's winter base.

"She ought to be all right in five or six days," Leroy told William Rudy of *The Blood-Horse* right after she was scratched from the Beldame. "We had leaned toward racing her next year, and on what we know now there seems to be no reason why she can't run. The chip seems to be an old one, she may have had it for months. If you X-rayed all the horses in America, you'd probably find most of them have had chips."

In December 1980, Bert told the *Daily Racing Form*, "(Jolley) will see how she does when he sends her back to work. If she is 100 percent right, we'll race her as a four-year-old. If not, it's likely she'll be brought to Kentucky and bred."

He said they were considering three sires for her first mating: Spectacular Bid, Honest Pleasure, and Secretariat. "Spectacular Bid and Honest Pleasure were both outstanding racehorses, and as for Secretariat, we've had a lot of luck with him, particularly with General Assembly," Bert said.

Breeding Secretariat to Genuine Risk had both practical and romantic angles. The practical side was that Bert owned a share in Secretariat, bought when Seth Hancock syndicated the stallion for Penny Chenery

Tweedy in February 1973. Later that year Bert had been there when Secretariat galloped off by thirty-one lengths to take the Belmont Stakes and sweep the Triple Crown.

The romantic overtones to a mating between Secretariat and Genuine Risk were immense. Never had two Kentucky Derby winners been bred to each other. The resulting foal would be virtually priceless.

But beyond the thoughts of how much a foal from Genuine Risk might be worth were the feelings the Firestones had for the filly. Being intensely private people, the family did not readily reveal their feelings toward Genuine Risk to the public.

The Firestones, especially Diana, had a deep love for Genuine Risk. Despite the filly's fierce competitiveness on the track, Genuine Risk was a sweet horse in the barn. The family had grown very attached to her, and she, in her way, had become a member of the family. None of the Firestones could pass her stall without dispensing a treat.

At the end of the year, Genuine Risk won the Eclipse Award as outstanding three-year-old filly, defeating fellow nominees Love Sign and Bold 'n

Determined. It must have been a strong temptation for Diana and Bert to retire Genuine Risk on that high note. But, as when she won the Derby, the Firestones elected to race on.

During the winter of 1981, LeRoy gradually brought Genuine Risk back into shape in Florida. The Gulfstream Park backstretch workers enjoyed having a celebrity in their midst, and often grooms and hot walkers would drop by the stall to meet her.

Besides rest, Genuine Risk had had no treatment other than trimming the foot on the affected leg.

The filly was entered in two races in early 1981, but LeRoy scratched her when the track came up muddy both times. Training went along well until February 23 when the filly injured her right front hoof in a work-out at Gulfstream. She tore a piece of the frog in that foot and required about a week's rest.

With no lasting ill effects from the frog injury, Genuine Risk moved with her stable to Hialeah for the meet there. The third week of March, she breezed five furlongs in 1:01 2/5 seconds. Shortly thereafter, LeRoy shipped Genuine Risk back to New York.

The chestnut filly had grown and matured over the

winter. What hadn't changed about her was the look in
her eye that said "I never quit."

After conferring with Bert and Diana, LeRoy
entered Genuine Risk in a $32,000 allowance race for
fillies and mares at Aqueduct on April 11. It would be
her first start in more than six months.

Prior to the race, LeRoy commented on the filly in
The Blood-Horse. "She has matured physically the way
you'd want her to. She has put on some weight, is
quite a bit heavier, and I don't want her to get any
heavier than this. But she was somewhat delicate last
year, and this year she will have to carry more weight,
I suppose, so it's good. The thing is, you never can be
sure just how they will come back, whether she'll have
that same old spirit."

One thing Genuine Risk did have was Jacinto back
in the saddle for the seven-furlong race.

Cheers and applause thundered from the old grandstand at Aqueduct as the pair swept under the finish
line by more than nine lengths in 1:22 4/5. Bettors had
created a minus pool on the race, wagering $407,744
of the total show pool of $432,401 on her. Minus pools
occur when the track or betting parlor takes in less

money on a bet than it has to pay out. Genuine Risk's minus show pool ended up totaling $75,869.12. Genuine Risk was definitely back, and racing fans and bettors showered their approval as she stood in the winner's circle.

Her next race came on May 25 at Belmont in another allowance, this one worth $35,000. It was Genuine Risk's first, and only, start on the turf, and Don MacBeth was in the saddle.

Jacinto alleged he did not ride Genuine Risk in this race and her subsequent one because of a disagreement with LeRoy. The jockey said he had angered LeRoy after refusing to ride an untalented mount in his stable. He is, however, philosophical about it. "Jockeys are like baseball players; you don't feel sorry for the team you left when you play for another team." Although the filly ran well, she weakened toward the end of the mile and one-sixteenth race. Carrying 121 pounds, she finished third behind Smilin' Sera and In Rhythym. Genuine Risk had given away eleven pounds to the winner and four pounds to the runner-up.

LeRoy kept the filly in training at Belmont and then moved her to Saratoga when the fabled upstate track opened its summer meet. The Firestones and LeRoy made up their minds to point Genuine Risk for the grade I Woodward Stakes, against the colts, on September 5. If all went all, they would continue to the grade I Marlboro Cup on September 18.

To prepare for the Woodward, Genuine Risk was entered in a seven-furlong allowance for fillies and mares on August 10. Jockey Jeff Fell substituted for Jacinto and got along well with the filly. Fell had watched how Genuine Risk ran in her other starts and thought he had a feel for how she liked to be ridden.

Under 119 pounds, Genuine Risk blew away the field, winning by eight and a quarter lengths in 1:21 2/5.

But Fell and the filly weren't finished. They galloped out the mile in 1:34 3/5, giving the filly a solid workout for the Woodward.

The team moved back to Belmont, and Genuine Risk continued working toward the Woodward when a freak accident ended the filly's career. Genuine Risk escaped from her hotwalker one morning and ran into a fire hydrant, injuring her knee, Bert recalled in late 2002.

Although the injury was not considered serious, the Firestones decided at the time not to take any chances.

They regretted the turn of events but looked forward to racing their champion filly's offspring.

LeRoy also was sad to see her go, but remembered feeling some relief. "I felt like I was guarding a national treasure while she raced as a four year-old. I lived in fear that something would happen to her," he recalled in 2003. "You know, she had nothing left to prove."

Not on the track, in any case. The Firestones had always intended for Genuine Risk to return home once her racing career ended. And that is what happened. The filly was shipped to Catoctin Stud in Virginia while the Firestones decided to whom she would be bred.

CHAPTER 10

A Royal Pairing Followed By Disappointment

Genuine Risk was shipped to Waterford Farm in Midway, Kentucky, to prepare for her new life as a broodmare. Dr. R. Smiser West and his son, Bob, operated Waterford, and both were consummate horsemen.

In a strange quirk of circumstance, Bold 'n Determined was sent to the same farm, and the mares ended up in adjacent stalls. The former rivals soon became friends. "I'd come up here at night and they'd be rubbing noses at a hole in their stalls at the water bowl," Bob West told Maryjean Wall of the *Lexington Herald-Leader*. "I'd say to them, 'What are you talking about?'"

Bold 'n Determined was bred that first season to Exclusive Native, Genuine Risk's sire. Genuine Risk was going to Secretariat, so fans would get their hoped-for mating of the Derby winners.

But Bert downplayed the "romance" in such a match by taking a more realistic view.

"There's no guarantee a foal by Secretariat and Genuine Risk will be a champion. We hope it will. It would be great if we could have a Triple Crown winner out of that combination," Bert told Dave Kindred of the *Washington Post*. "Secretariat is the best racehorse I ever saw. A big, strong, neat horse. Genuine Risk isn't big, but she's neat, too...We think it's a great breeding."

In February 1982, television crews filmed Genuine Risk as she left Waterford Farm for her "date" with Secretariat at Claiborne Farm in nearby Paris. John Sosby, manager of Claiborne Farm, realized the historic implications of the breeding.

"You know, it was a great moment in racing history," he told the *New York Post* the day after the breeding. "It's something you add to the list of things you've seen and will never forget. You were there when it happened."

About thirty-five people witnessed the breeding. "If I had made (the event) public, they'd have probably had to put up a guard on the gate to keep traffic out. As for Genuine Risk...well, sometimes young, maiden mares right off the track can be very high strung and excitable. But she was one of the best. She took it like a veteran, like she knew what she was there for. Everything worked right. Everything was perfect."

At the time of her breeding to Secretariat, Genuine Risk was just one of eight fillies in history to have won a Triple Crown race. Prior to Genuine Risk, only three of this group of fillies were bred to classic winners. With the exception of Nellie Morse, the 1924 Preakness victress, these fillies, unfortunately, did not turn into great broodmares.

Regret, the only other filly to have won the Kentucky Derby before Genuine Risk, was never mated with another Derby winner. She was, however, bred twice to 1918 Belmont winner, Johren. Although neither foal was a champion on the track, both became successful broodmares.

Tanya, the last filly to gallop to victory in the Belmont (in 1905), was mated with Rock Sand, the 1903 English Triple Crown winner. That breeding resulted in Tan II, who won nineteen of 128 races.

It was the breeding of Nellie Morse and American Flag, the 1925 Belmont winner, that truly produced another champion in Calumet Farm's Nellie Flag.

Nellie Flag won the 1934 Matron Stakes, Selima Stakes, and Kentucky Jockey Club Stakes and was named champion two-year-old filly that year. Nellie Flag also started as favorite for the 1935 Kentucky Derby but finished fourth behind eventual Triple Crown winner Omaha.

The mating of Nellie Morse and 1928 Kentucky Derby winner Reigh Count (who also sired 1943 Triple Crown winner Count Fleet) produced the good handicapper Count Morse, who in 1937 rolled to victory in four handicaps: the Clark, Great Western, Blue and Gray, and Ben Ali.

Genuine Risk was pronounced in foal after her breeding to Secretariat. She was then shipped back to Catoctin Stud in Virginia to await the birth of her foal. And along with her, racing fans waited anxiously for eleven months to pass.

The Firestones and the farm staff were impatient to see Genuine Risk with her first foal. Although Genuine Risk was a celebrity in the world of racing, she was a favorite at the farm because of her kind nature. The pregnancy was uneventful, and no one could have predicted the misfortune to come.

On April 4, 1983, at two in the morning, Genuine Risk was three weeks past due when she went into labor. The delivery was difficult, but she finally produced a strapping chestnut colt. Any relief over the birth was short-lived. Catoctin Stud employee Buck Moore was there for the birth and knew right away the colt was dead.

"She (Genuine Risk) got up fine. She'd look at the foal and then go away. Then she'd come back and look at it again and go away. Mares will nicker for a foal to get up. She did that. Then what they do is what she did. What they do is begin to cover it up. They'll shove the straw over it to cover it up. She did that. She knows. Then I took the foal," Buck stated in the *Washington Post*.

Buck called Bert to tell him the news. Bert was so shook up he could not go back to sleep that night. Bert's assistant Susan Grant was left to read a statement tearfully to members of the press who phoned.

"Genuine Risk delivered a stillborn chestnut colt at 3:10 a.m., April 4. She was three weeks overdue, which is a common occurrence, and this tragedy was completely unexpected. The mare is doing fine and has suffered no ill effects.

"Mr. and Mrs. Firestone have announced they will now breed Genuine Risk back to Secretariat this year. Previously, they had planned to send her to Nijinsky II, which they will now do in 1984. The Firestones thank all those who were so interested in this foal and are very sorry to announce this loss."

Seth Hancock of Claiborne Farm made it possible for the Firestones to breed back to Secretariat. Bert had already used his 1983 season to breed another mare. Hancock generously switched a stallion season with the Firestones, enabling Genuine Risk to be sent back to Secretariat. Hancock would instead breed to Nijinsky II, the 1970 English Triple Crown winner.

"I can understand the Firestones wanting to fulfill this historic breeding and I'm happy to arrange it," Hancock told the *New York Times'* Steven Crist. "We're all terribly sad here, but when you get into the breeding game, you have to expect things like this."

Bert and Diana received thousands of sympathy cards from racing fans, expressing deep sadness at the loss of the colt.

Within weeks Genuine Risk was shipped back to Kentucky to be mated again with Secretariat. Despite the best efforts of the farm, she did not conceive. There would be no foal in 1984.

Bert stated that sometimes "when a mare has a stillborn foal it often takes a year or two before they conceive again. It didn't come as a big surprise when she didn't conceive again (on the second breeding)." What Bert and Diana didn't realize at the time was that it would be many years before Genuine Risk would carry to term a foal that would survive.

Genuine Risk was bred to The Minstrel, a son of Northern Dancer, in 1984 but was never pronounced in foal. Bert and Diana decided to send Genuine Risk to their farm in Ireland, Gilltown Stud. She would be bred to Cure the Blues in 1985. Cure the Blues was bred by and raced for the Firestones, winning the 1980 Laurel Futurity.

Unfortunately, after two matings with Cure the Blues in 1985, Genuine Risk did not become pregnant. Sent back to America, Genuine Risk was bred to Dixieland Band at Lane's End Farm in 1986. No foal resulted from this union either as the mare aborted in the first trimester. An unhappy pattern was emerging, one that would haunt the Firestones and the public

equally. In both 1987 and 1988, Genuine Risk again aborted foals in the first trimester.

In 1989 she carried a Cure the Blues foal for eight and a half months, but the fetus then died. In 1990 she was in foal to Dixieland Band again and aborted. She then aborted again in 1991 and 1992.

Some veterinarians felt that Genuine Risk's first tough labor with the big stillborn Secretariat colt had compromised her fertility. Others guessed that her racing career had somehow affected her ability to bear a live foal. But when it came right down to it, no one really knew why she was unable to carry a live foal to term.

Bert and Diana moved Genuine Risk to Three Chimneys Farm in Midway, Kentucky, on June 15, 1990. Although the results were not instantaneous for the Firestones, moving Genuine Risk to Three Chimneys Farm would change their luck, and Genuine Risk's.

GENUINE RISK

CHAPTER 11

A Genuine Reward

Manager Dan Rosenberg of Three Chimneys Farm knew it would be an uphill battle to get his famous charge to carry a foal to term. He had followed the mare's struggles through the years and hoped he could help the Firestones attain the dream of a live foal.

"We had a long-standing relationship with the Firestones," Rosenberg said. "They called and asked if we could take her, and we were happy to say yes."

Genuine Risk arrived at Three Chimneys in June of 1990. She would remain for more than eight years.

Success took a few years. In a 1992 interview with *Daily Racing Form* writer Linda Souyak, Dan talked about Genuine Risk's problems. "There's no pattern as to why and when she aborts. One year she lost the foal between 60 and 70 days. Another year she carried the foal six months and then aborted. She even carried a foal to near full-term once, but it was stillborn, dead from a twisted umbilical cord. It's just bad luck."

Bert and Diana decided to breed Genuine Risk to Three Chimneys' stallion Rahy. A foal of 1985, Rahy had raced in England as a two- and three-year-old. At four he had competed in America, winning the grade II Bel Air Handicap.

Rahy's sire was Blushing Groom, who also sired Arazi, Nashwan, Blushing John, and Rainbow Quest. His dam was the great race mare Glorious Song, who had won more than one-million dollars and was 1980 Canadian Horse of the Year. Rahy would become one of the great stallions of the 1990s, fathering such horses as champions Serena's Song, Fantastic Light, and Noverre, plus stakes winners Tranquility Lake, Early Pioneer, Exotic Wood, and Tates Creek.

Although the mating of Genuine Risk and Rahy would not attract the fanfare that her mating with Secretariat had, it was a tremendous blending of blood-lines. And for the anxious Firestones, it would end a long quest and the heartaches they had endured.

Genuine Risk was bred to Rahy twice in the spring of 1992. An ultrasound examination thirteen days after the second breeding found three embryos. The next day the smallest one was "pinched" (eliminated). During the scan the day after that, two embryos still existed, and the smaller was pinched.

It was important that Genuine Risk only carry one embryo, as twins in horses are very dangerous to the health of the mother. It is also risky for the twins, as it is rare that twins will be carried to term and survive.

Despite the elimination of the second embryo, Dr. Richard Holder of the Hagyard-Davidson-McGee veterinary clinic in Lexington did not feel optimistic that Genuine Risk would produce a live foal. "The odds are not good. If she were a younger mare, you might say she'd have a shot, but I don't expect her to carry this one to April (1993)," he told *Daily Racing Form*.

Holder believed her troubles stemmed from her first stillborn foal and the difficult delivery, a problem known as dystocia. "The ironic thing about Genuine Risk is that she gets pregnant rather easily but cannot carry to full term. I've never had one like her," Holder remarked.

Bucking the odds, Genuine Risk held the pregnancy through 1992 and into 1993. Genuine Risk was now sixteen years old and had yet to feel a foal nurse. The staff at Three Chimneys was now holding its collective breath.

The public was also anxious for the birth, thanks to an article by Joe Durso that ran in the *New York Times* just a few weeks before Genuine Risk was due to foal. In the article, Dan Rosenberg dreamed ahead to what he hoped would happen.

"I've had things that were thrilling in my professional life," Dan told the *Times*. "Things that were enormous triumphs. But to call Diana Firestone and tell her she's got a live foal would be the greatest thrill."

Dan had high expectations of Genuine Risk as a mother. "She's very sweet and gentle, and shows good instincts for motherhood. And we're monitoring her carefully. The foal's heartbeat is fine. We check the amniotic fluid. Everything we can monitor is within normal parameters." That was soon to change.

On May 15, 1993, Genuine Risk's veterinarian, Dr. Jim Becht, decided to induce labor. Checking her that afternoon, Becht had discovered that the foal's heart rate was abnormally slow and arrhythmic. He worried about the chances for the foal if they waited and quickly acted to hasten the process.

Genuine Risk was whisked to the famed Rood and Riddle Equine Hospital in Lexington, along with Three Chimneys' broodmare manager Gary Bush and two members of his staff, Joey Mattingly and Tom Clark.

At Rood and Riddle the delivery went smoothly and quickly for Genuine Risk. Although the colt's heartbeat was irregular at first, it soon became normal. A pretty chestnut colt had entered the world, and Genuine Risk was ready to be a mother. She nickered to her foal as it struggled to its feet. By late that night, the new mother was back in her stall at Three Chimneys Farm with her colt.

The relief among the staff at Three Chimneys was palpable, for even Dan acknowledged that he did not think Genuine Risk would produce a live foal. The next day Three Chimneys announced to the world that the long wait was over, both for the mare and the people who loved her. "It's a Boy!" the farm proclaimed.

Cards and letters poured into Three Chimneys, some just addressed "Genuine Risk, Kentucky, USA." Others were more formal and directed to "Mrs. Genuine Risk and Son, Midway, Kentucky." Carrots and roses for Genuine Risk streamed into the office. Dan fielded

phone calls from dozens of television stations wanting to come to the farm and shoot footage of the mare and foal. The birth had taken on a life of its own.

"A real cross-section of America was interested in Genuine Risk and her first foal," recalled Dan. "It was truly a human interest story. I was very surprised. She touched so many people for so many different reasons. For me personally, it was a relief that she finally had a colt. A major relief! The whole world was watching, and I dreaded facing her fans with bad news again.

"I also experienced great joy that she had finally done it. With every new foal, there are the hopes and dreams that they carry. But for this foal, it was even more than that."

Over the years many childless couples identified with Genuine Risk's plight. "They all related to the struggles this mare endured to have a foal. It gave them a bit of hope," said Dan.

Two days after his birth, the foal needed to go back to the veterinary hospital. He had developed two impactions of the colon that needed surgery. Within a day, he was back with Genuine Risk. Everyone collectively exhaled.

Ten days after he was born, the striking chestnut and white colt and his mother received a visit from the Firestones. Diana was very excited, and could not get enough of looking at the pair. "Look at how happy she is," Diana said to *Daily Racing Form* writer T.L. Thomas about her great mare. "If Genuine Risk could talk, she'd say, 'Oh, my happy day.' " It was hard to tell at that point who was truly happier, Genuine Risk or Diana.

Genuine Risk proved to be a good mother, attentive and caring. Perhaps it was the years she had spent looking at other mares with their foals that prepared her for motherhood. Now, she would have her own foal to care for.

The public could not get enough of Genuine Risk and her newborn colt. Bert told *The Blood-Horse*, "One thing about Genuine Risk was that she was a star. She got the public enthused about racing. I think we need more of that. I'm glad to see she's gotten so much publicity. At the farm, they've gotten hundreds of letters from well-wishers and people who remembered Genuine Risk when she was running, and even from school kids who didn't remem-

ber. I think that's what the sport needs — more stars that people can relate to."

A name was needed for the colt, and soon the farm was fielding fifty calls a day from people with suggestions. In the end the name the Firestones stuck with made the most sense. Genuine Risk had earned her Genuine Reward.

Genuine Risk did not conceive in 1994, and Diana brought her to Virginia so her doting owner could see her every day and ride her on occasion. The mare returned to Kentucky for a 1995 breeding to the Firestones' grade I-winning homebred stallion Chief Honcho. In the spring of 1996, she had another colt. Like Genuine Reward, this colt was bright chestnut with flashy white markings.

Even though the second colt's birth did not receive as much fanfare as Genuine Reward's, the Firestones were just pleased that the foal was delivered safely. He was aptly named Count Our Blessing, for the gifts Bert and Diana felt they had received from Genuine Risk.

"We are thankful for the two foals Genuine Risk had; Genuine Reward by Rahy in 1993 and Count Our

Blessing by Chief Honcho in 1996," Diana said. "Both colts for various reasons did not race."

The year after Count Our Blessing was born, Genuine Risk carried a foal to term. The veterinarians performed a Caesarean on her, but the foal, a filly, did not survive, according to the Firestones.

During the years that Genuine Risk resided at Three Chimneys Farm, Diana would often visit with her. The bond between the two had grown stronger over the years.

"Diana went to the farm to be with her," Dan said. "Diana would bring her carrots and would get a lead shank and hand-graze her. They just liked being together."

The Firestones announced Genuine Risk's official retirement from breeding in the winter of 2000. She was twenty-three years old, and her time as a brood-mare had passed. Genuine Risk left Three Chimneys for the Firestones' Newstead Farm in Virginia.

Dan supported the decision to retire Genuine Risk. "She'll be well cared for and loved by Diana in Virginia. Those two are attached to each other.

"Genuine Risk was one of the gutsiest fillies that

ever raced," he added. "There's no question about that. It takes an exceptional filly to beat the colts like that. She belongs in the history books."

And so she is.

EPILOGUE

Enduring Heroine

S ally Humphrey and her husband, Watts, still breed Thoroughbreds to sell at auction. While Genuine Risk was Sally's only major success as a breeder, she has been associated with other good horses through her husband and his family. Watts and his aunt, Pamela Firman, bred 1985 Belmont Stakes winner Creme Fraiche, and Watts and Lane's End Farm owner William S. Farish bred 1987 Breeders' Cup Distaff winner Sacahuista.

Sally still insists it was beginner's luck when she bred Genuine Risk. But even so, a plaque marks the stall in which the 1980 Derby winner was foaled at Shawnee Farm.

The Humphreys' daughter Vicki has pursued the family passion for Thoroughbreds. She and her husband, Phil Oliver, train in Florida and New Jersey.

The man who foaled Genuine Risk, Al Cofield, continued to work for Sally and Watts. For thirty years, from 1955 until he retired in 1985, Al handled the foaling of almost every horse at Shawnee Farm. He passed away in 1989 at the age of seventy-eight.

Bert and Diana Firestone have been through some up and downs since Genuine Risk helped earn them an Eclipse Award as outstanding owners in 1980. In October 1981 their relationship with LeRoy Jolley ended.

"We were together for ten years, a long time for a relationship to last in this business," Jolley commented. The Firestones wanted LeRoy to be their private trainer, but he didn't like the idea. "I've never been a private trainer for anybody."

In 1986 popular horseman Bill Mott signed on as the stable's private trainer, a relationship that endured until 1992. Mott had a successful run with the Firestones, and in 1986 the stable earned more than four-million dollars. Stakes winners under his tenure included Eclipse Award-winning turf horse Theatrical, Chief Honcho, Take Me Out, and American Chance. The Firestones also bred Paradise Creek, champion turf horse of 1994.

In addition to flat racing, the Firestones have enjoyed success in steeplechase racing. Their horse Jimmy Lorenzo won the 1988 Breeders' Cup Steeplechase and was named champion steeplechaser that year.

Bert Firestone was also active in the business world. During the late 1980s and early '90s, he owned Florida's two largest racetracks, Gulfstream Park and Calder Race Course, but sold them after a brief tenure.

The Firestones endured several controversies during the 1990s, including a costly lawsuit involving their Irish farm, Gilltown Stud.

Despite a dispersal of some of their horses in 1992, the Firestones remain active in Thoroughbred racing and have horses in training in France, Ireland, and the United States. They continue to buy horses at auction.

The couple, who several years ago moved their base of operations to Newstead Farm just outside of Upperville, Virginia, also remain extremely active in the horse show world. In 1998 Diana was presented with the American Horse Shows Association's (now USA Equestrian) Walter B. Devereux Trophy, given to a person who exemplifies the ideal of good sportsmanship.

Bert and Diana spend a good deal of time traveling the world to watch their youngest daughter, Alison, compete in the glamorous world of show jumping. Alison, a frequent member of the U.S. Equestrian Team, hopes someday to win an Olympic gold medal in her chosen sport.

Matt Firestone lives in Wellington, Florida, but has a small breeding operation in Kentucky. He sells about a half-dozen horses a year at auction, where he also keeps an eye out for a nice horse to buy.

Matt checks in on Genuine Risk once or twice a year. "Considering her age, she looks great. She has a good life."

Continuing the Firestone legacy, Matt's son, Kent, now twelve, accompanies him to auctions. Kent particularly likes the Keeneland sales and anxiously waits for the catalogs. Daughter Christina, now seven, rides all the time, and younger son, Oliver, eighteen months old, has already been on a pony. Matt's wife Sylvia runs her own business developing polo ponies.

Susan Grant, Bert's assistant from 1976 to 1989, now works as Matt's assistant. She began working for Matt in 1997. "I've loved horses since I was a little girl," Susan said in 2003. "The romance of racing is what I love. Racing has a romance that a lot of people don't understand."

LeRoy Jolley, inducted into the Racing Hall of Fame in 1987, had other good horses after Genuine Risk, including Manila, the 1986 champion male turf horse, and Meadow Star, the 1990 champion two-year-old filly.

LeRoy still trains and has fifteen horses at the Palm Meadows training track in Boynton Beach, Florida. His sons, Leroy Jr. and Tim, assist him at the track. His daughter, Laura, has worked for him as secretary on and off through the years.

He last saw Genuine Risk right before she foaled Genuine Reward. "She looked wonderful and had carried her age extremely well. In fact, it looked like you could take her back out and run her!" Genuine Risk remains one of his favorite horses. "You're only going to get a few like that in a lifetime. I was very lucky to have her."

Jacinto Vasquez was inducted into the Hall of Fame in 1998. In addition to being the regular rider for Genuine Risk, he also rode Ruffian, Foolish Pleasure, Princess Rooney, Forego, Risen Star, Manila, and Smile during his successful career. Retired from racing in 1996 after riding more than five thousand winners, he lives outside of Ocala, Florida. Jacinto now works for Carl Bowling, who has farms in Ocala and in Palestine, Texas. He exercises horses and helps break yearlings.

"Jacinto was probably one of the greatest riders ever," LeRoy recalled. "He won a high percentage of stakes races. He was also great at breezing horses and getting them ready for the big races." LeRoy used him as a jockey until Jacinto retired.

Many people have asked Jacinto over the years to compare the two famous fillies he rode to glory, Ruffian and Genuine Risk. In 1980 he said in *Sports Illustrated*, "I won't compare Ruffian to Genuine Risk. I never will." He has stuck to his word.

Along with the glories on the track, Jacinto also ran into controversy. The New York State Racing and Wagering Board suspended him from riding for one year in the mid-1980s for allegedly offering a bribe to fellow jockey Eddie Maple in 1974. He denied the charge.

Following his comeback in 1985, he spoke with Craig Wolff of the *New York Times* about the charges. "There's a black spot on my name. I worked hard for my name for many years. And I have my family to face. I won't stop fighting until the truth is found and I clear my name."

Angel Cordero Jr., the rider for Codex, retired from race riding in 1992. By that time he had won three Kentucky Derbys, two Preakness Stakes, and four Breeders' Cup races. Over his career he rode such great horses as Seattle Slew, Slew o' Gold, All Along, Chief's Crown, Life's Magic, and Spend a Buck.

Surprisingly enough, Matt now calls Angel Cordero one of his friends. Even Sally Humphrey has a soft spot for him.

"After the Preakness I thought I'd never want to see Angel Cordero again," Sally remembered. "Then something happened that same year that changed my mind. I took the kids that spring to Keeneland for some racing, and it was very cold and wet, just a miserable day. Watts (Watts III) didn't have fun. His whole picture of racing was that you would be cold and wet when you went to the track.

"Later that year I took the kids to Saratoga. It was an absolutely beautiful day, and we had lunch on the porch. Watts didn't want to leave the porch because he thought he would be cold — that was what racing meant to him.

"Then, our horse didn't run well. Watts just wanted to go home. He was sitting quietly and kind of moping in a corner. I looked over and there was Angel talking and joking with him. Angel saw a young kid who wasn't having fun at the track and took it upon himself to cheer the child up. During each post parade, Angel waved 'Hi' to him. What Angel didn't know was that the young boy he cheered up was Watts. Angel didn't know who Watts was, but he decided to make an effort so that a child would have more fun.

"I walked up to Angel later in the day and told him that the child he helped was Watts. I also told him 'I thought I'd never forgive you.' But it was hard to stay mad at Angel after that."

Jack Jackson, Genuine Risk's groom, still works on the backstretch at Belmont Park in New York. A few years ago, Jackson stayed in New York when LeRoy moved to Florida. "Jackson's health is not good," LeRoy shared. "New York has a good backstretch health care program, so he elected to stay at Belmont." All in all Jackson worked forty-five years for the Jolley family.

Dan Rosenberg continues as manager at Three Chimneys Farm. He still marvels that he was part of Genuine Risk's life. "To ever be around a horse like this, you're very, very privileged. Genuine Risk was just plain different. It's like she was in another league from another planet. All the great ones have that 'feel' about them — Seattle Slew, Secretariat, and yes, Genuine Risk. I've been around a lot of very, very good horses. When you are in the presence of greatness, you know it. She was one of them."

He says that Genuine Risk still gets mail at Three Chimneys. Several times a year he hears from people asking about Genuine Risk and Genuine Reward. "Of course, the perfect ending would have been for one of Genuine Risk's colts to win the Kentucky Derby. They were both nice colts, but it was not to be."

Genuine Reward was sold by the Firestones and now lives in Wyoming after standing at stud in Virginia. As a stallion, Genuine Reward had his first winner when Top Reward took a claiming race on June 2, 2001, at Pimlico. Despite his breeding, Genuine Reward has been a disappointment at stud. Like Genuine Reward, Count Our Blessing did not race.

John "Buck" Moore continues to work for the Firestones and, coming full circle, once again takes care of Genuine Risk. He and his wife, Shirley, live at Newstead Farm in a house just about sixty feet from the broodmare barn that Genuine Risk calls home.

"GR," as Buck likes to call her, has remained in good health. "She gets two square meals a day and all the hay she wants. She's got her own stall when it gets too hot or too cold, and she gets quite a few visitors every year. GR loves attention, and you better have candy with you, preferably mints or Tic-Tacs. She loves anything candy-like. Carrots are another favorite." Personality-wise, Genuine Risk is "a bit more docile now than when she was a yearling."

Helping Buck look after Genuine Risk is Dr. Calvin Rofe, the Newstead Farm veterinarian, who has a special fondness for the mare.

Genuine Risk is sound despite the left knee she damaged at age four. She can still gallop as fast as her legs will carry her. "She definitely rules the roost," Buck laughed. For close to seven years, Genuine Risk had been turned out with Farnley Trilby, one of Alison's old show ponies. Genuine Risk and Farnley

Trilby were best friends and did everything together. The pony passed away in the summer of 2002.

Buck didn't wait for GR to mourn. "I know it affected her some, but she didn't show much depression. I put her out right away with some other horses so she would have something else to think about."

Genuine Risk is still the only filly to have contested all three legs of the Triple Crown. During her career, she never finished worse than third, a remarkable accomplishment. At times it seems history has overlooked her, but accolades have still come her way.

Although she was not born in Virginia, she was admitted to the Virginia Thoroughbred Association's Hall of Fame in 1981. In 1986 she was inducted into the Hall of Fame at the National Museum of Racing in Saratoga Springs, New York.

Since 1984, the grade II Genuine Risk Stakes has been run at Belmont Park every spring. Contested at six furlongs, the race has showcased many marvelous fillies and mares. The legendary Safely Kept won the race from 1989 to 1991. Most recently, Eclipse Award winner Xtra Heat, a bargain auction purchase for five thousand dollars, added to her legend and pocketbook with a win in the 2002 running.

An honor of another kind was in store for Genuine Risk in 2002. Breyer, the company that manufactures plastic model horses, added a limited edition model of her. Released as part of a set of three Breyers called the "Ladies of the Bluegrass," the set contained Genuine Risk, Regret, and Winning Colors, the three fillies who captured the Kentucky Derby. (Ironically the mold used to depict Genuine Risk was originally used as a model of Ruffian.) The offering sold out quickly, and it is very difficult to find the model of Genuine Risk.

Through the years artists and photographers have been inspired by her athletic prowess and gentle beauty. Richard Stone Reeves and Fred Stone have both painted her, and Eclipse award-winning photographer Barbara Livingston has focused her lens on the mare.

Genuine Risk's more enduring legacy, however, is with the fans, particularly girls and young women. Genuine Risk brought a whole generation of female racing enthusiasts into the sport.

Mention her name, and scores of women can tell you exactly where they were when Genuine Risk won the Derby. They will also share how their hearts were broken when Genuine Risk's Secretariat colt was stillborn.

To this day, Genuine Risk engenders a sense of abiding love and deep respect in racing fans, both male and female. She was a hero to them in 1980, and she remains a hero to her fans today.

GENUINE RISK's
PEDIGREE

	Native Dancer, 1950	Polynesian / Geisha
Raise a Native, 1961		
	Raise You, 1946	Case Ace / Lady Glory
EXCLUSIVE NATIVE, ch, 1965		
	Shut Out, 1939	Equipoise / Goose Egg
Exclusive, 1953		
	Good Example, 1944	Pilate / Parade Girl
GENUINE RISK, chestnut filly, 1977		
	Migoli, 1944	Bois Roussel / Mah Iran
Gallant Man, 1954		
	Majideh, 1939	Mahmoud / Qurrat-al-Ain
VIRTUOUS, b, 1971		
	Zucchero, 1948	Nasrullah / Castagnola
Due Respect II, 1958		
	Auld Alliance, 1948	Brantome / Iona

GENUINE RISK's RACE RECORD

Genuine Risk ch. f. 1977, by Exclusive Native (Raise a Native)–Virtuous, by Gallant Man

Own.– Mrs B.R. Firestone
Br.– Mrs G.W. Humphrey Jr (Ky)
Tr.– Mrs Leroy Jolley

Lifetime record: 15 10 3 2 $646,587

Date-Track	Cond/Dist	Times	Class	Running line	Jockey	Wgt	Odds	SR	Finish (order)	Fld
10Aug81-1Sar	fst 7f	$:22^4:45^2 1:09 1:21^{2\!/\!3}$	3↑ⒺAlw 32000	3 2 1hd 11 16 18^{1}_{4}	Fell J	119	*.10	95-15	Genuine Risk$119^{8\frac14}$Clown's Doll$117\frac12$Samarta Dancer$119^{3\frac34}$	4
		Ridden out mile 1.34 3/5								
25May81-6Bel	fm $1\frac{1}{16}$①	$:24^3:47^4 1:12 1:42$	3↑ⒺAlw 35000	5 2 $31\frac12$ $1\frac12$ 1hd 3^2	MacBeth D	121	*.40	84-12	Smilin'Sera$110^{1\frac13}$InRhythm117^{nk}GenuineRisk121^{no} Weakened	6
11Apr81-7Aqu	fst 7f	$:24^3:45^3 1:10^1:22^4$	4↑ⒺAlw 32000	2 4 $22\frac12$ $2\frac12$ 17 $19\frac12$	Vasquez J	122	*.10	87-22	GnuineRisk$129\frac12$BacktoStay$110^{2\frac14}$Justacam114^{nk} Ridden out	5
27Sep80-8Bel	fst $1\frac18$	$:48 1:12^2 1:36^4 1:49^1$	3↑ⒻRuffian H-G1	1 5 $3\frac12$ 31 31 1no	Vasquez J	118	*.50	81-19	GenuineRisk118^{no}MistyGallore124^{nk}It'snthAr$118^{5\frac34}$ Driving	6
10Sep80-8Bel	fst 1	$:23^2:46^1 1:10^4 1:35^2$	3↑ⒻMaskette-G1	2 4 45 31 1hd 2no	Vasquez J	118	*1.20	91-22	Bold'nDetrmind122^{no}GnunRsk$118^{6\frac14}$LovSgn$120\frac12$ Just missed	5
7Jun80-8Bel	my $1\frac12$	$:50^1 1:15^1 2:04 2:29^4$	ⒻBelmont-G1	1 5 53 $2\frac12$ 22 2^2	Vasquez J	121	5.10	69-17	Temperence Hill126^2Genuine Risk$121^{1\frac12}$Rockhill Native126^2	10
17May80-9Pim	fst $1\frac{3}{16}$	$:47^4 1:11^1 1:36 1:54^1$	ⒻPreakness-G1	5 6 44 $43\frac14$ 21 $24\frac12$	Vasquez J	121	*2.00	94-12	Codex$126^{4\frac34}$GenuineRisk$121^{2\frac34}$ColonelMorn126^7 Bothered turn	8
3May80-8CD	fst $1\frac14$	$:48 1:12^4 1:37^2 2:02$	ⒻKy Derby-G1	10 7 $74\frac34$ $11\frac12$ 12 11	Vasquez J	121	13.30	87-11	Genuine Risk121^1Rumbo126^1Jaklin Klugman126^4 Driving	13
19Apr80-8Aqu	fst $1\frac18$	$:47^2 1:13^1 1:37 1:50^4$	ⒻWood Memorial-G1	3 3 32 $31\frac12$ 32 $3\frac12$	Vasquez J	118	8.20	79-17	PluggedNickle$126^{1\frac14}$ColnlMorn126^{nd}GnunRsk$121^{2\frac34}$ Game try	11
5Apr80-7Aqu	gd 1	$:23^4:46^4 1:12 1:38^3$	ⒻHandicap 35000	4 4 32 31 $32\frac12$ $31\frac12$	Vasquez J	124	*.20	73-20	GenuineRisk124^2TellaSecret$115^{3\frac34}$SprucPn113^{11} Ridden out	4
19Mar80-7GP	fst 7f	$:22 :44^4 1:09^4 1:22^3$	ⒻAlw 17000	3 5 44 $32\frac12$ $1\frac12$ $12\frac12$	Vasquez J	113	*.40	91-20	GenuineRisk$113^{2\frac34}$SoberJig$112^{3\frac34}$PeaceBells$115^{1\frac12}$ Ridden out	6
17Nov79-8Aqu	fst $1\frac18$	$:48^1 1:13^1 1:38^3 1:51^1$	ⒻDemoiselle-G2	6 4 $3\frac12$ 2hd 2hd 1no	Pincay L Jr	116	1.20	79-21	GenuineRisk116^{no}SmartAngle$121^{6\frac34}$SprucePine$112^{3\frac34}$ Driving	7
5Nov79-8Aqu	fst 1	$:23 :46 1:10^2 1:36$	ⒻTempted-G3	4 5 $51\frac14$ $11\frac12$ 12 13	Vasquez J	114	*.90	86-18	GenuineRisk114^3StreetBallet$117\frac12$TellScrt$114\frac34$ Ridden out	9
18Oct79-6Aqu	fst 1	$:23 :47 1:11^4 1:36^2$	ⒻAlw 15000	6 2 21 2hd 12 $17\frac12$	Vasquez J	115	*.60	84-18	GenuineRisk$115^{7\frac12}$GoingEast117^5CintoTora$115^{4\frac12}$ Ridden out	6
30Sep79-4Bel	sly $6\frac12$f	$:23 :45^2 1:11^2 1:18$	ⒻMd Sp Wt	8 11 45 $46\frac12$ 23 11^3	Vasquez J	118	*3.10	86-24	GenuineRisk118^{13}RemoteRuler118^{13}Espadrille118^{13} Driving	11

Led, gamely

Index

Photo Credits

Cover photo: (Kinetic Corporation)

Page 1: Genuine Risk at Saratoga (Catherine Magnuson); Genuine Risk head shot (Barbara D. Livingston)

Page 2: Exclusive Native (Tony Leonard); Raise a Native (The Blood-Horse); Virtuous (Milt Toby); Gallant Man (Bert and Richard Morgan)

Page 3: G. Watts and Sally Humphrey, et al. (Anne M. Eberhardt); Shawnee Farm barn, Genuine Risk nameplate (Tom Hall)

Page 4: Bert, Diana, and Alison Firestone (Anne M. Eberhardt); Matthew Firestone (Anne M. Eberhardt); LeRoy Jolley with Genuine Risk (Bob Coglianese); Jacinto Vasquez (NYRA)

Page 5: Genuine Risk's first race (Kim Pratt); Winning the Tempted Stakes (Bob Coglianese); Winning the Demoiselle (Bob Coglianese)

Page 6: Third in the Wood Memorial (NYRA); Genuine Risk grazing at Churchill Downs (Milt Toby)

Page 7: Genuine Risk leading in Derby (*Lexington Herald-Leader*); Winning the Derby (Kinetic Corporation); Derby winner's circle (Milt Toby)

Page 8-9: Genuine Risk at Pimlico (Dell Hancock); Genuine Risk and Codex in the turn (Wide World Photo); Codex winning Preakness (Dell Hancock); Belmont post parade (Barbara D. Livingston); The Belmont finish (Bob Coglianese); "The Lady is a Champ" sign (Milt Toby)

Page 10: Genuine Risk and Bold 'n Determined (Bob Coglianese); Genuine Risk winning the Ruffian (Bob Coglianese)

Page 11: Genuine Risk getting new shoes (Bob Coglianese); Genuine Risk working (NYRA)

Page 12: Winning her four-year-old debut (Bob Coglianese); Working on the turf (NYRA); Genuine Risk in Saratoga paddock (Kim Pratt)

Page 13: Genuine Risk with Genuine Reward (Anne M. Eberhardt); Diana Firestone with Genuine Risk and Genuine Reward (Anne M. Eberhardt)

Page 14: Genuine Risk with Count Our Blessing (Anne M. Eberhardt); Count Our Blessing at Laurel Park (Kim Pratt)

Page 15: Genuine Risk as pensioner; head shot (Barbara D. Livingston)

Page 16: Regret (Keeneland-Cook); Winning Colors (Kinetic Corporation); Genuine Risk (*Lexington Herald-Leader*)

Dedication and Acknowledgments

I dedicate this book to my sister Hope Barry and to my husband Thom.

Numerous people provided help in writing the story of Genuine Risk: the Firestone family; Sally Humphrey; LeRoy Jolley; Jacinto Vasquez; Susan Grant; Candace Lovinger; John "Buck" Moore; Dan Rosenberg; Tom Gilcoyne of The Racing Museum and Hall of Fame; Chris Goodlett of the Kentucky Derby Museum; Kim Pratt; Barbara Livingston; Tom Keyser; Debra and Michael Lischin; Kathy Schwartzman; Jane White; Dana Ray; Jeanne Wood; Mary Hilton; Eric Connolly; Hope Barry; Siobhan McGowan-DeLancey; Lisa Cheney; Steve Price; Karen Anderson; DVM; and Kate Rogers.

I relied on written accounts of Genuine Risk's races and stories about her team from many periodicals including *The Blood-Horse*, *Daily Racing Form*, *The Horsemen's Journal*, and the *Lexington Herald-Leader* among many newspapers. Three books were helpful for background details, Jane Schwartz' *Ruffian: Burning from the Start*, William Nack's *Secretariat: The Making of a Champion*, and John McEvoy's *Great Horse Racing Mysteries*.

H ALLIE McEVOY was born in Greenlawn, New York, just a short drive from Belmont and Aqueduct on Long Island. She began riding as a child and has owned horses her whole life. The first race she saw was the legendary meeting of Desert Vixen and Susan's Girl in the 1973 Beldame Stakes at Belmont.

A member of the International Alliance of Equestrian Journalists, McEvoy has covered a range of horse sports including show jumping, eventing, dressage, reining, and racing. Her articles and photographs have appeared in *The Horse: Your Guide to Equine Health Care*, *Equestrian Magazine*, *Dressage Today*, *Horse Sport*, and *L' Année Hippique* among many other publications.

McEvoy is the author of two previous books, *Showing for Beginners* and *Horse Show Judging for Beginners*. Additionally, she is a licensed horse show judge for USA Equestrian.

McEvoy and her husband, Thom, also an author, breed Thoroughbreds for the track in New York State. They live in Bolton Valley, Vermont, with many cats and dogs.

Available titles
in the

THOROUGHBRED
Legends®

series:

Man o' War

Dr. Fager

Citation

Go for Wand

Seattle Slew

Forego

Native Dancer

Nashua

Spectacular Bid

John Henry

Sunday Silence

Ruffian

Swaps

Affirmed/Alydar

Round Table

War Admiral

Exterminator

Secretariat